Uncertain Truth

Frederick Sontag

University Press of America, Inc.
Lanham • New York • London

Copyright© 1995 by
University Press of America,® Inc.
4720 Boston Way
Lanham, Maryland 20706

3 Henrietta Street
London, WC2E 8LU England

Library of Congress Cataloging-in-Publication Data

Sontag, Frederick.
Uncertain truth / Frederick Sontag
p.   cm.
Includes bibliographical references.
1. Belief and doubt.   2. Certainty.   3. God--Proof.   I. Title.
BD215.S66   1995
121'.6--dc20   94-46769 CIP

ISBN 0-8191-9850-1 (cloth: alk paper)
ISBN 0-8191-9851-X (pbk: alk paper)

⊖™The paper used in this publication meets the minimum
requirements of American National Standard for Information
Sciences—Permanence of Paper for Printed Library Materials,
ANSI Z39.48–1984.

For

Jo and Doris, Bill and Muriel, John and Lyn

and their children

Happy the gentle:

they should have the Earth

for their inheritance.

Mathew 5:4

The Jerusalem Bible

iii

Other Books by Frederick Sontag

Divine Perfection: Possible Ideas of God, 1962

The Existentialist Prolegomena: To a Future Metaphysics, 1969

The Future of Theology: A Philosophical Basis for Contemporary
Protestant Theology, 1969

The Crisis of Faith: A Protestant Witness in Rome, 1969

The God of Evil: An Argument from the Existence of the Devil, 1970

God, Why Did You Do That?, 1970

The Problems of Metaphysics, 1970

How Philosophy Shapes Theology: Problems in the Philosophy of
Religion, 1971

The American Religious Experience: The Roots, Trends and the
Future of American Theology (with John K. Roth), 1972

Love Beyond Pain: Mysticism Within Christianity, 1977

Sun Myung Moon and the Unification Church, 1977

God and America's Future (with John K. Roth), 1977

What can God Do?, 1979

A Kierkegaard Handbook, 1979

The Elements of Philosophy, 1984

The Questions of Philosophy (with John K. Roth), 1988

Emotion: Its Role in Understanding and Decision, 1989

The Return of the Gods: A Philosophical/Theological Reappraisal of
the Works of Ernest Becker, 1989

Forthcoming   *Wittgenstein and the Mystical*
The Descent of Woman
The Acts of the Trinity

Table of Contents

PREFACE

We have in fact   for some time been living in a Post-Modern age. Just as science led us into the Modern Age with its revolutionary promises, so science, particularly theoretical physics and its cosmologists, have led us out. Philosophers, theologians, intellectuals, just as they lagged behind science in pioneering the Modern era, so now seem to be the last to respond to the revolution stemming from vastly speculative, fascinating but uncertain, scientific postulations. Theologians in particular feared the Modern Age as being destructive to religious faith, and so it tended to be. But just as they fought it long after it was generally accepted as reigning theory, so now they have clung to the optimism of Progress and Finality long after revolutions in scientific theory have led us into uncertainty. This important change is not such that it makes religious faith necessary (that would contradict the meaning of 'faith'), but it is at least possible and may even at times be appropriate.

Freud revolutionized our outlook on ourselves and raised the prospects for psychology to the level of promulgating a universal theory, offering us a now widely available human cure to human ills. Yet Darwin in biology represents an even more dramatic Copernican revolution in our outlook on our world and on God. Early modern science and psychology seemed to eclipse God. But whereas none of the Rationalists could establish 'God' as necessary and universal (those prime characteristics of Modern thought), Darwin's view of our 'descent' seems to fit in more easily with cosmological schemes of our planetary origins. This opens the door to a creative, to an uncertain God, but one no less powerful, to preside over the vast unleashing of forces in which we live that are nowhere near so neat in plan as Augustine imagined or hoped.

'Truth' must, therefore, be reconceived in its philosophical perspective. It should be divorced from an old, now-unreachable ideal of certainty. This does not mean that we must abandon truth to skepticism or to a debilitating relativism; we can maintain it as truth nevertheless, even though uncertain. Skeptics arise when an inflexible demand for truth-absolute proves unobtainable. 'Belief' is possible without rigidity and seems more appropriate to a volatile time, one which so long ago abandoned the certainty of control anticipated by

Modern Age optimists. 'Facts', we now must admit, are often quite distant from the truth we seek, as every theoretical physicist knows. The foibles of human inconsistency and even perfidy, which once seemed to be left behind, have returned along with terror and destruction. If Marxism-Leninism was the hallmark of truth made certain, powerful, and revolutionary, its recent internal self-destruction now requires us to "see" truth differently.

As we deal with one another as human beings, one problem of assessing truth is that we so often face dishonesty and deception. And this personal situation is not at all distant from the way philosophers should reconceive truth, since it is not divorced from us in hermetically sealed purity, untouched by human weakness. Rather, it shares in our foibles. Truth seems not to have been found where the Modern Age thought it would be, neither in an adulation of the methods of science nor in a strict Rationalism or Empiricism. Our problems proved to lie on more obscure levels, where they are less able to be detached from emotion. 'Truth' is connected to our emotional life, for good and for ill, because we are just as dependent on its power to achieve insight as we are to lash out in destruction. The royal road to truth, so attractively imagined, has in fact led us to uncertainty, but to 'truth' nonetheless even if more vulnerable than we hoped -- if we will but accept it for what it is.

Chapter I. TRUTH AND THEORY

A. FREUD AND UNIVERSAL THEORY

It is well established that Freud wished to develop a 'universal' theory, one that could not only be applied to all human beings but which would be confirmed by all practitioners and used as a confident base to relieve the suffering of man (and thus of women). Those who follow the way he developed psychoanalytic theory in his career know that he began with physiological research. Could he have found a material base for human neurotic symptoms, he might have achieved his goal. But he could not. Later, when he lectured to medical students he warned them that his theories would seem 'strange', since medicine trained them to "think physically".

Yet his goal still might have been achieved if all clinical practitioners had used their case studies to confirm his theories about the dynamics of the unconscious. In spite of the massive and pervasive influence which his thought has had, no one argues that his theoretical constructs can be confirmed universally or used to outmode all other theories about the human psyche. Why? We should look at the process of theory formation itself for one clue.

The 'paradox' we face is that theory itself is not 'physical' or seen, and its very formation is often not physical and universal but rather creative, individual and so subject not to necessity but to the contingencies of the freedom of the human mind. This origin does not in itself fault out any theory's potential universality, but it means that any important theory must always be applied beyond its origination. So we must ask about the status of 'theory' itself and its relation to the human mind. If it is a contingent creature, as all theory is and particularly that about the mind/soul itself, is it "infected" from its origin by an instability which makes it unable to operate necessarily?

Moreover, is the new insight that leads to theory formation itself in turn dependent on the life and times of its originator, so that both its structure and its resulting insight are in fact based on the larger cultural/intellectual climate of that day? To say this is not to suggest the ultimate in "historical reductionism" but to try to explain how new postulates comes to be accepted and to be effective, just as Freud's eventually were. Theory is not a fact in the world but is a creative product of the human mind.

Does following Freud through his search for insight and his eventual theory formation, plus his changes in it as it advanced, give us any insight into the nature of theory, its powers and its vulnerabilities? How can theory be both effective and fragile? Exploring Peter Gay's biographical account is illuminating[1]. If it was Freud's fate to "agitate the sleep of mankind" (p.xvii), how is it that some theories can do this and others not? The answer cannot lie with their "obvious truth", since we know that truly revolutionary theories are anything but obvious to the innovator's contemporaries and are even puzzling, more often than not, to the theorist him/herself. *The Interpretation of Dreams*, Freud's "great life discovery", we know proved to be of little general interest for some time.

"Insight such as this falls to one's lot but once in a life-time," we know he stated (p.4). If true, why was it so long in being recognized, and what enables or facilitates its recognition when finally it comes? We know it to be Freud's thesis that "distorted memories are no less, possibly even more, revealing than accurate ones" (p.83). If so, just as psychoanalysis claims for its foundation, and as the *Interpretation of Dreams* documents, 'truth' can never be a surface phenomenon, never obvious. Thus, probably it can never be universal, since its referent remains unseen and often even "counter-factual".

---

[1] Gay, Peter. Freud, Anchor Books, Doubleday. New York, 1988.
All page references are to this edition.

This is recognized to be largely true in mathematics and in physics today, but Freud inaugurated 'esoteric' truth for the psyche. In any literal sense, then, theories can neither simply explain nor correspond to 'facts' or empirical data. They may of course be indirectly confirmed, although never beyond replacement. Theories may provide enlightenment regarding former puzzles (e.g., the unconscious processes). But that has been the claim for 'esoteric' doctrines all along; they are prized by the few who understand. They cannot by their nature become exoteric. True, Freud thought his theories could achieve universal acceptance, but he did not fully understand the insubstantial -- if important -- status of the theory he developed. He wrongly saw it as an extension of research in physiology.

Freud was attracted to Darwin's theories, which in itself is telltale. We can better understand this when we move next to examine something of Darwin's theory formation, which is even more non-factual in its back-ground than Freud's. Freud, who reports that "as a young man I felt a strong attraction toward speculation and ruthlessly checked it" (p.85), ironically could not quite see the speculative quality under-girding his own theory formation. This confusion of insightful theory with truth itself, we will argue, is the Achilles heel of the Modern Age's self-conception. To think that theory can become truth is the hubris of that era which must be corrected.

Freud feared that he would lose himself in the "morass of speculation" (*Ibid.*), which is a danger. But an awareness of theory's fragile nature is, ironically, better protection against this than claiming greater solidity for the theory than its quixotic nature can support. "The physical-mathematical method" seemed to Freud at first to be the only way to approach 'inexplicable' phenomena. But when his research forced him to abandon that for verbal forms, he still held out the notion of "final explanation" which the Vienna positivists had thought achievable. He seems never to have realized that words as symbols can never achieve the finality of mathematics, and that in fact therein lies their power.

If Freud was started on his road to discovery by abandoning literal explanations ("that a bit of truth lurks behind every popular lunacy" (p.57)), how could such insight ever have been thought capable of universality? To seek out psychological causes for psychological effects, rather than neurological, is to abandon the direction of physical evidence and to come closer to the insight offered by literature, something Darwin (and Jung) saw but Freud did not. 'Listening' became for Freud a method, a privileged road to knowledge which his patients mapped out for him. But the ear can never have the directness of the eye. It can reveal, we know, but never absolutely.

If dealing with the human unconscious is like "the technique of excavating a buried city" (p.71), we clearly see the likeness and the differences: (1) What lies hidden is exposed; but (2) these are not the stones and pots of archaeology; the contents of the unconscious are not physiological structures and so do not yield a confirmation of a theory about that which is exposed. Oddly and ironically, what Freud thought would confirm scientific rationalism, due to its universal confirmation, reverses itself and becomes the crucial factor in forever separating truth from theory. The theory about the life of the unconscious can never be reduced to fact. Even the fact that 'cure' results does not prove the theory 'true'. Healing and health may not be due simply to the 'truth' of the theory employed.

'Free association' we know to be Freud's discovery and his developed technique. But nothing so uncontrolled can ever be reduced to a fixed technique. It seems to depend more on aesthetic intuition than on rational processes. The twin aim of psycho-analysis was to provide therapy and to generate theory (p.74). This happens. But the therapeutic technique or success, we know, does not generate one universally confirmed theory but in fact something more like a creative explosion of theories. The ramifications of psychoanalysis that reach into every sphere of culture are undeniable. But such energy is centrifugal rather than centripetal where theory is concerned. This may produce 'truth' of an unorthodox variety, but it defies systematization.

The goal of a "natural-scientific psychology", one that would represent psychological processes as "quantitatively determined states" (p.79), is gone. As a consequence, 'psychology' in order to become more of a 'science' retreated to experimental and statistical measurement, away from the unconscious and the theory needed to deal with it. If Newton has been superseded in physics, the attempt to subject the laws of the mind to the laws of motion has gone with it, but so also must any simple equation of 'truth' with empirical data. Truth, which to the Modern World seemed so close, has receded, like God, into a "learned ignorance". We certainly know more, but we have also learned more about what we do not -- and perhaps cannot -- know.

"Self-analysis", which Freud thought necessary in order to begin the "science of the mind" impartially, becomes a symbol of our dilemma concerning truth. We know in retrospect that Freud's own self-analysis was never completed and never fully satisfactory. As Plato said about creating the ideal Republic, to achieve an ideal you must begin by "scraping the canvas clean". But if the canvas upon which truth is to be written as scientific is even partly unconscious, you can never complete the process and so cannot be sure of being rid of all distortion on the part of the theory former. Theory is subject to the flaw of the original sin in its birth; that is the modern meaning of 'Genesis'.

"There are no marks of reality in the unconscious", Freud reports (p.94), and so there is no way of distinguishing between truth on the one hand and emotionally charged fiction on the other. The fact that a "cure" is achieved does not tell us that our operative theory is distortion free. We know that 'positivists' got rid of emotion by relegating it to 'psychology' vs. 'philosophy'. Such an artificial narrowing of the field of inquiry can be carried out for those who accept it. But we surely cannot claim that this yields 'truth' in any comprehensive sense, because we have blocked out the chief source of our uncertainty and puzzlement. If fairy tales enshrine buried truth, as Freud recognized, they cannot be literalized, or at least perhaps not without destroying their revelatory power, as Jung later commented.

"True self-analysis is impossible, else there would be no illness", Freud remarked candidly (p.96). But then there is no neutral starting point for theory construction. 'Dialogue' becomes the patient-analyst technique for discovery, but Plato, who codified the method, felt that is was at once revelatory but also incapable of finality. The unending analysis, which many patients experience, confirms this at least partially . Virgil's quote, which Freud admired, is fitting: "If I cannot bend the higher powers, I will move the infernal regions." (p.125). But if for the mystics God lies beyond articulation, "the infernal regions" of the mind may be ultimately chaotic as well as beyond rational reduction.

If dreams give us 'messages' but not the ones the eager lay public expects, any 'translation' of these will be subject to the same disputes that plagues all evaluation in literature. Some interpretations establish themselves as at least temporarily preferable but never so as to be beyond replacement by a new literary theory. The key notion

Freud used, "wish fulfillment", cannot become "a universal law of dreams" (p.107), as he wished, since their very nature prevents final, single interpretation, important as dreams may be. Freud develops the theory of 'distortion' and the distinction between 'manifest' and 'latent' dream content. Censorship and conflict are rife and pervasive. But can the "crazy logic" eventually be reduced to system?

Freud admits that no dream can ever be interpreted exhaustively. The riddle cannot wholly be cleared up (again, like God, the "higher power"). If so, then the theory about it, as well as about the structure and the dynamics of the unconscious, can never be finalized either. Freud thinks that theory formation can be held free from the uncertainties inherent in its material. But that is to assume that the formation of the theory can itself at least sometimes be generated free from uncertainty, thus creating certainty from itself. But that Cartesian dream was based on the supposed clarity of consciousness; it did not take into account "the infernal regions" in the psyche which defy theory's finality.

B. TRUTH AS FICTIVE

"When it is first advanced, theory is at most fictive"(p.3), Gillian Beer tells us.[2] And she gives us a remarkable account of how Darwin developed his destabilizing theory, while setting it in the context of the literature of his time. She illustrates the way in which Darwin's theory, as it emerged, bears similarities to the development of the plot of a novel. Her contention is that, in its formative stages, a new theory is in a real sense 'fictive'. But where theory and truth are concerned, our more important question is: Does a theory, any theory, irremovably at its core retain an illuminating similarity to fiction? We know by their popularity that millions of intellectually sophisticated people find both dreams and fiction a genuine source of insight, as Freud and Darwin illustrate.

Philosophy has been linked with aesthetic forms, in Sartre's plays, in Camus' novels, in Heidegger's use of poetry, but first of all in

---

[2] Darwin's Plot, ARK Paperbacks, Routledge and Kegan Paul, London, 1985.
All page references are to this edition.

Plato's Dialogues. In our search for truth, is it self-deception to think that philosophy can oppose itself to aesthetic forms and achieve a greater clarity and certainty? Is it an intentional irony that Plato is thought to want to censor the poets, all the while his own philosophical form does not allow for direct statement of truth either? Darwin writes neither plays nor dialogues, yet given the role literature played in his theory formation, can we discern anything from him about the nature of theory and its distinction from truth?

If major scientific theories "rebuff common sense", as Beer claims (*Ibid.*), the hope to verify theory empirically seems lost in a romantic past. "They [novel theories] call on evidence beyond the reach of our senses and overturn the observable world." (*Ibid.*). Any revisionist theory, such as Darwin's, never represents the world as it is currently perceived. The consequences of such a theory go far beyond what its framer usually conceived. Narrative can provide "a fiction by which to read the world" (p.4). In what sense does theory, even the most profound scientific theory, occupy a similar status? We may overlook this fact simply because our culture is dominated by evolutionary paradigms. Thus, we miss the imaginative power in Darwin's theory which is ingredient in all revolutionary theories. His theory has been naturalized by us.

Reading *The Origin of Species*, Beer tells us, involves you in a narrative experience; it is both subjective and literary (p.5). She quotes Richard Ohmann: "To state something is first to create imbalance, curiosity, where previously there was nothing, and then to bring about a new balance" (p.6). Can this be said both of literary artists and theorists in any field as well? First of all, in Darwin's time science had not been divorced from literary discourse; scientific texts could be read very much as literary texts. So perhaps the specialization that has come into the language of scientific (or philosophical) theory has, although touted as an advantage, cut us off from recognizing just how much of the power of any novel theory stems from (must stem from?) its comparison to a literary text.

The process of narrative is concerned with time and change; so is evolutionary theory. Thus, it has affinities to the problems of fiction (p.7). If so, this may help us to understand the status of fiction, the role it plays, and particularly why no theory achieves finality or is immune to being revolutionized. How much is the problem of appraising the effectiveness of theory, and its eventual instabilities and uncertainties, like understanding how a work of fiction achieves classical status -- but then is in turn altered in style by a new insightful generation? Evolutionary theory is first a form of imaginative history. It cannot be empirically demonstrated effectively. "So it is closer to narrative than to drama", Beer reports (p.8).

Plato in the *Timaeus* told us his account of creation and said that all accounts of creation must remain as "likely tales". They may be illuminating, but they are ultimately beyond final confirmation. All the implications of evolutionary theory do not point in one direction; thus its imaginative power. Its contradictory elements serve as a metaphorical base. "Darwinian theory will not resolve to a single significance nor yield a single pattern" (p.9). The power of the theory lies in its suggestiveness, Beer reports, which is certainly true of Darwin's. But this prohibits finality and singularity of interpretation. Its power stems from the uncertainty, which eventually will allow it to be superseded, just because it offers suggestions beyond its simple statement.

The Rationalists, even the Empiricists, had operated on the assumption that Nature was designed on a plan leading toward unity, unity of thought due to unity in design. Darwin, taking a clue from literature in his time, saw incredible multiplicity, even waste, and it was this which fascinated him, rather than the drive toward simplicity. This confounds 'design' theories, or at least it does so if one operates on the assumption that design involves simplicity and avoidance of loss. Darwin focused on loss and extinction (God's errors?) which he saw as all around him in our human descent. That is why it is so crucial that he uses the term 'descent', whereas metaphysician-theologians had for centuries talked in terms of 'ascent' toward unity, always away from multiplicity.

Plotinus, for instance, knew full well that the creative descent from the One led toward multiplicity and matter. But he and countless others went on to assume that human effort should be spent retracing our descent by ascent, moving away from multiple origins and up to where purity and thus our "salvation" lay. Darwin focuses, on the other hand, on multiplicity as the key to Nature's creative activity. Our appearance on the scene is not neat; it is not governed by principles of the conservation of energy or of simplicity. It seems wasteful, if still marvelous, in the variety of its production: Darwin is a precursor to 'chaos' theory, which is not itself 'chaotic', just illusive for the "neat and tidy" prediction-bent rational mind. Theology is revolutionized. The order and explosion of descent becomes more central to comprehending our place in the world than the order of ascent, which so long had been assumed to be the path to increased human understanding.

'History', when it became a dominant and controlling interest, connected itself to notions of Progress. When tied together with Modern science, the Present came to be seen as our high point. Authority was located there, just as many in the nineteenth century thought (p.13). Reversing this, evolution "does not privilege the present" (*Ibid.*). Our thought is directed back, to centuries of gigantic struggle hidden from present view, just as Freud challenged consciousness by postulating the seat of human thought and action to lie out of view in the unconscious. For Freud access to its secrets, its deciphering, lay in a hidden past. Of course, for Freud this was found only in a personal, biographical past. However, Jung extended this, paralleling Darwinism, to the full extent of our human past, which remains never fully visible.

Not only is visual sight threatened, which with its emphasis on present experience was stressed by Empiricism, but our fascination grows over reaches of existence that lie beyond the domain of reason, beyond any direct confirmation. This is similar to contemporary physics and astrophysics, which deal with the present order as only explainable by a vast drama beginning far from present sight. There is a fascination with an "oceanic richness" which expressed itself "in the use of symbol typical of Victorian prose" (p.14). Freud was educated by Victorian fiction; Darwinism inspired us to use symbol and metaphor, whereas the Modern World thought it would leave behind the imprecision of these forms of speech for more precise, definitive forms of thought. Darwin needs imprecise forms of expression. He both adds a dramatic challenge to the Modern World's rejection of classical/medieval forms of thought while at the same time setting the stage for exploding the simplicity which the Modern World sought.

Does Darwin, then, condemn us to imprecision and force us to locate the understanding of ourselves and of our present order in an always partially hidden past? Yes, exactly: evolutionary theory challenges our use of present experience to understand the past. What we see before us may be clearer, more accessible to us, but it is no longer a fully useful model. Understanding, instead, lies closed away in a near inaccessible, very distant past. This is open to speculative postulates which are partially conformable, but results are mostly accepted due to their spread of intellectual illumination. 'Light', that ancient symbol of insight, returns as the philosophical paradigm, replacing 'experience' and even 'reason' as our chief touchstone. If God is no longer the Sphinx which will not yield divinity's final disclosure, then our ancient past, one both physically, psychologically, and biologically quite unlike our present state, now holds the key to the understanding of ourselves and of Nature; yet it defies our demand for finality.

The individual, that center of Modern hope and celebration, cannot be understood alone but only in connection with a long line in the development of the species. Moreover, the coveted belief in 'Progress', Hegel's conviction that his time in Berlin was a peak of culture, is threatened when 'degeneration' and 'retrogression' appear to be equally necessary laws of development (p.15). True, Hegel's historical dialectic does not proceed smoothly. Negativity and the "slaughter bench of history" dictate loss along the way. But Hegel held to a confidence that nothing is wasted, nothing is unnecessary; all is "taken up" and conserved in our advance. This is a romantic outlook which Whiteheadians still preserve today, in spite of holocausts.

Greater and greater complexity took over, thus defeating the hope for simplicity and unity, since complexity and waste is what evolutionary theory thought it saw behind all apparent present fixity in Nature. The issue is not so much whether a God can be the author of this vast and tangled show, but whether the complacency of our desired fixity of understanding is placed beyond hope. We may still be dealing with a divinity, but it is not a very comfortable, easy creator. Evolution speaks more like a thunderous Jahweh than like a God of love who sacrifices to save us. Jesus could not possibly be the "logical outcome" to Darwin's creative process. True, he can still be postulated as a revelation of God's "secret purpose and plan", but not as the culmination of the drama we find outlined in an evolutionary Nature. "Natural Theology" based on Darwin is a dead end. Such a God could not write the Gospels.

But in its place Darwin does offer us "a total system for understanding the organization of the natural world." (p.16). It is all-inclusive, whereas Jesus offers only a limited, even if attractive, anti-natural focus. 'Difference' and 'multi-fariousness' are operative in evolution, so that the recent use of 'difference' as an interpretive category is in fact expressive of "Nature's plan". Mathematics, the darling of Positivism, cannot capture the picture of our world as it evolved. All things cannot be number, as Pythagoras and countless followers have hoped. In philosophy symbolic logic is sidelined as a restricted sphere, its elegance fascinating but reflective neither of the world's processes nor of human production, insofar as we reflect our origins in our present behavior. The springs of explanation are hidden from direct view and from simple formulation.

Evolutionary theory is born in a tension which neither it nor those who follow it can escape. It is inclusive in its scope, which every Modern wanted, but it is at the same time based on profusion and variety, thus defeating simplicity and finality. Evolutionary theory comes to function like a myth, breeding metaphor and paradigm (p.17), and it does so just at a time when we hoped to escape dependence on myth for our understanding. However, Jung had noted our dependence on myth to illuminate the unconscious, a power which he goes on to exploit. Freud actually wanted to move beyond myth to fact, although he did not manage that escape. Evolutionary theory does hold out the promise for a system because of its all-inclusiveness. But what it offers with one hand it takes back with its dependence on literary style. True, we humans seem not to be at the center of Nature's design, but if we could only fix it all in one final theory, we might still prove to be its masters.

However, in its framework evolutionary theory suggests that we are "not fully equipped to understand the history of life on earth" (p.19). Freud struck our rational optimism from below, although he wrongly thought he had also cracked the secret code; Darwin hits at rational optimism and our hoped for enlightenment from the distant past. Feuerbach wanted to change theology into anthropology. The study of man replaces God as the center of the Modern World; fine. But if Darwin knocks us out of the center of Nature's concern, our self-investigation a la Descartes or Freud becomes a castle built on sand, about which Jesus warned us. The center of our theory formation is destabilized, long before 'deconstruction' argued for it on cultural, intellectual grounds.

Emerson had used the whole of nature as a metaphor for man's mind. But this 'congruity' is lost if 'nature' has in fact proceeded as Darwin divined, because either that is not how our minds work or, even if it should be discovered to be so, then rational finality, clarity, and distinctness (the gods of Modernism) are not possible but only illusory. They are phantoms of a mind bent on enclosing itself in its own understanding. "What is man that aren't mindful of him?" takes on not a sense of wonder but a quality of awe mixed with terror. Our resources are not perfectly fitted either to our intellectual or to our spiritual task, since all that we must take in, in order to explain ourselves, lies outside our possible domestication. The limit of our observation is too narrow. Observation and sense experience will not suffice (p.21).

Dramatically opposing Descartes and all the Rationalist tradition, Claude Bernard argued that "man does not possess within him the knowledge and criteria of things outside himself" (as quoted by Beer on p. 21). Descartes dominated his time, because it was hubris-feeding to believe his proposal for certainty. Darwin and evolutionary theory quietly oppose this, until at last the non-finality of scientific theory is recognized and pulls the foundations out from under Descartes' astonishing ego-centerdness. Present consciousness is unaware of its important evolutionary past, just as it is unaware of what lies beneath itself in the unconscious, whether individual or collective. The past could not have been governed by a rational, even dialectical progress, as Hegel hoped.

Empiricism worries over the comprehension of our present sense impressions. Logicians worry over technical paradox and the imprecisions they face. Rationalists seek increased comprehension of known material. But evolutionary theory obliges us to study a world in which we are largely absent and whose detail we can never reduce to present knowledge. What we must try to understand is a domain where we are not. Thus, evolutionary theory alienates us from ourselves, makes us aware of 'nothingness', that experience which Existentialists so stress in their rebellion against rational system building. The Nothingness central to Zen enlightenment is also introduced into the middle of what was for some time a growing sense of human power and intellectual optimism. Our position as observers becomes "essentially unfavorable" (*Ibid.*).

Evolutionary theory turns out to be both threatening and exhilarating. "The living world is neither open to man's observation nor related to him." (p.22). Old problems, once hopefully bypassed, return: Chance, death, survival. And the powers of technology and science cannot solve them, save to speed us on to more elaborate forms of speculation. If our environment is not as stable as we thought, our understanding has no fixed frame either, or at least it is not a simple, present, final one. Unforeseeable and uncontrollable change become inescapable. Prediction is not firm; chaos theory is anticipated, anti-essentialism prefigured.

We do not face a "great chain of Being" but more an "inextricable web of affinities". Such structure has a looseness which strict rationalists will deplore. Lamarck had proposed "a world of intelligent desire rationally satisfied." (p.24). In Freud's terms that now becomes a dream based on wish fulfillment, precisely because the real world refuses us that satisfaction. The language of intention does not fit evolutionary theory, and Phenomenology has tried to see all thought as intentional. That may be so, but against the backdrop in Nature our thought proves unsupported as not central to a developing world. Is 'will' a force for change? If not, Nietzsche is grounded in his flight toward the Superman. What if the world is not 'intelligible', in the Rationalists sense, or cooperative, in the Hegelian or Marxist sense?

If the speed of change increases, as Darwin suggested was possibly the case (p.25), what we see before us, and the rational frameworks we employ, can neither be taken for granted nor accepted as stable. Nietzsche is right in one sense but questionable in his suggestion that we are or ever can be in control of our transformation. Prometheus must be summoned back to return our appropriated fire to the gods. We did not make our world; we possibly do not control its development, although we may observe it with growing wonder. Early in his life Darwin was fascinated by fear, astonishment, and the intensity of paradox (p.29). He did not need to read Kierkegaard. The power of invention fuels his passion for discovery, but it was not a search for simple facts. Everything cannot be "just what it is and not another thing", else we misunderstand Nature.

For Malthus, 'fecundity' was a danger to be suppressed. For Darwin, "fecundity was a liberating and creative principle", (p.34), but its variability and potential for change threatens simple rational comprehension. Diversity and profusion are important, not simplicity. Superabundance is natural. Imaginative pleasure is a means to understanding, vs. a restriction to either reason or the senses. But this defies finality. Metaphor is necessary; it is not rendered obsolete, else reality cannot be adequately expressed. Language needs to be expressive to be truthful, not rigorous and clear. Poetry is a key, not a distortion, as Heidegger will later argue. Analysis and logic ironically carry us further away from an ability to grasp Nature's Reality. Mobility is the norm, rest its opposite, form its temporary result. The language of science cannot, should not, in the end be different from the language of life.

The aim to please readers, as well as to disturb and to unsettle them, is vital to Darwin (p.39). In that sense his is a return to the classical Socratic task: Questioning every security. When is a vague expression more accurate than precision? This is an irreducible question. Meaning inheres in activity and in interrelations, Darwin believes, echoing Pragmatism in advance. We live in a doubly profuse world, haunted by "an awareness of an unfathomable past whose individualities are wholly lost, and rarely human"(p.34). This is a "scientific theory" which upsets the projections of the Modern outlook, but it may in fact do more than Modern philosophy to explain the chaotic world we find before us still in our daily experience.

Flux and irretrievable loss govern "Darwin's plot", and these work more to explain twentieth century holocausts than Utopian projections. Natural objects generate their own laws. We are not governed from 'outside' nature. Foreordination would be an inappropriate divine instrument and would represent a total misunderstanding of the "new created world", as Heyden expressed it. 'Chance' as a creative factor is not peripheral, as Aristotle thought, but central. Chaos theory (which is not itself 'chaotic') is a better mirror to hold up to reality than Newtonian mechanics. The elements of the haphazard cannot be displaced. And ironically: Human presence is not ultimately eliminated from the center, although it is not at the center of an intentional creative design. Why not? Because the power of human imagination "is the only source of powerful interpretation" (p.44). Nature neither supplies this, nor allows itself to be read easily.

"Time implies an extended scale of existence beyond the span of our minds" (p.45). So Hawking's *A Brief History of Time* must be an imaginative construction, and its attraction to the non-specialized reader is more an evidence of its mythical and suggestive power than of his factual reporting. Language use, to be instructive, must have a real affinity with theory formation. Word choice is neither arbitrary nor totally optional, and it is never ours to construct at will. Like the poet, we must struggle to find the single best expressive term or symbol. Theory involves narrative ordering; such perception is crucial. Since the past can be played at any speed, one looks for the pace that is illuminating.

As we have said, although 'omniscience' cannot be an appropriate divine mode of apprehension, omnipotence is not displaced; it is only concealed. Divinity's hand cannot be read directly off of Nature, as theologians have claimed in hope. Divinity may have left its traces in our created evolutionary order, but these must border more on the mystical than on the obvious and involve a need for creative, literary expression. God cannot be the world's watch maker, nor the creator of the Rationalists' ordered systems, and certainly not Leibniz' "best of all possible worlds". Blake is closer to expressing the enigmatic power of creation than Descartes or Spinoza. Profusely various forms coexist; God did not create for Empiricism either. If the artist imitates God, as Shaftesbury thought, atonal music, cubism and abstract art may come closer to Divinity's form than Turner.

James Joyce writes ranging outward to infinity, defying overall simplicity of meaning. And the loss of theological ordering is at the core of "Darwin's plot". Scientific prose and literary prose either are not or should not be far apart. 'Location' is the only ordering principle. There is a sense that everything is connected, but these connections may be obscured. The reader of the novel and the scientific writer operate under an urgency to uncover such connections as they can express. Any dependency of one organic being on another is remote, not immediate. If God created man in his own image, this process tells us of a God different from our heart's desire, or about a process of creation that is far beyond simple replication.

Our dependency on God can only be distant, not immediate. Thus atheism is more 'natural' than belief, as Hume argued. Much that is in time and change lies between man and God. We are not just "a little lower than the angels" but light years in our descent, though no one denies that we may have angelic aspects, as well as demonic. Connections can be analyzed; the proof of what we discern is just never evident or immediate. Thus, theory is as much subject to change as was the order of species which we now find before us as fixed. The structure we observe is not any less fixed. Aristotle saw that right. It is just that its explanation is not fixed. Contemplation breeds not rest but our discontent with any present understanding. Revolutionary theories were long in coming, but they represent our increasing sense of non-fixity. However, any "easy" evolutionary doctrine simply misreads how difficult it is to produce a new form.

Woodsworth thought that "the eternal world is fitted to the mind" (p.49). Darwin does not deny this. Nothing else but our intellect is capable of forming theories. But his is a complex, non-obvious process, and any 'fitting' we postulate abhors finality in theory just as nature abhors a vacuum. A sense of mysticism descends on the natural world, because evolution gives us a sense of the incongruity and of the inefficiency of human reason. The workings of the world are never contained in Darwin's mind; he does not expect ever fully to understand them. Theory becomes necessarily hypothetical rather than inductive, which alone might have led to finality.

Darwin does not encourage us to settle on the small problems or on matters of detail. Nothing but the formation of a grand theory of design can help us to understand. Speculation is not a luxury to be abandoned, not an impediment, but a necessity for the survival of intelligence. From evolutionary struggles we learn how our body was formed to survive. Our intelligence must adopt the same mode of continual struggle if it is not to become extinct. We need not fight one another physically or necessarily struggle to outdo our competitors in order to survive in body. That is a popular misreading of the evolutionary model. We have already evolved. Now it is the mind which must struggle, not necessarily to evolve to a higher level as many Moderns thought, but simply to keep such insight we have achieved from fading away.

We often talk of 'describing' nature rather than interpreting it and think we get our clue from Darwin. But his "description" is figuratively based, his expression derived from creative literature, not from the periodic table. His medium of description is always language; it must be, but that does not mean it must be prosaic or literal. Language does control our apprehension of knowledge (p.51), but it can only be a flat or 'ordinary language' in unimportant instances. Darwin's words encompass a wide variety of meaning, and he does not analyze them. (Does analysis of language deaden our creative insight?) Manifest and latent plot operate for Darwin just as they do in Freud's interpretation of dreams.

His mode is not careful clarification but rapid summary and imaginative zeal (p.53). Symbols depend on human interpretive power, so theory cannot be objective and be effective. The natural order produces itself; no intervening creator is needed. But man the interpreter is. How, then, can language be "authenticated by the natural order"? (p.54). Never in such a way that further description, the revision or extension of theory, is not possible. There must be an "inherent heterogeneity of meaning and of ideology" (p.55) in all powerful theory. And this must be so, given our hidden and evolutionary past. There is no finality possible for our intellect, even if our physical bodies have achieved a stable outward form. Discussion always allows for contrary readings, as Plato's detractors often miss when they castigate him for a rigid orthodoxy of theory. Dialogue, discussion in our heterogeneous languages, does not allow finality.

We are "disqualified from observing the great movements of natural law" by the shortness of our life span (p.60). But ironically this should only redouble our efforts to understand. Evolutionary theory leaves us with a "learned ignorance", just as seeking God once did. However, through evolution we come to know a great deal more, but this 'learning' leads us to see more clearly all that we can never know with finality but still must seek. If we are made in the image of God, or if we are in kinship with nature, that all-pervasive kinship is not evident but hidden. God-linked we may be, but our "extended family" will not allow us to forget our lowly origins. Reversal is in order: We did not begin perfect in the garden and then fall into an uncertain state. We have been slowly emerging from that for ages beyond imagination.

Our origins are lowly, our potential high if uncertain and unstable. We are in a process of becoming. But in Heraclitus assertion of the dominance of flux, many miss the fact that there is no single logos to it which we can try to grasp and explain. To attempt this requires a constant activity; contemplation and rest are only "Aristotle's dream". He personifies nature as female, as passive. And since Nature fills the space left by God, Darwin may be seen as an early day feminist theologian, one who rejects passivity. But science has often been gendered as female, which some feminist critics of scientific theory have overlooked. Yet we never overcome the incongruity of the nature which surrounds us and our maladaption to understanding it. The internal and the external are always, "out of joint", as Kierkegaard observed too.

Nature has taken a delight in accumulating contradictions in order to remove the foundations from any theory of a pre-existing harmony between the external and the internal worlds, Darwin tells us. Leibniz is disproved, if we but look outside the mind and escape from our monad. Kierkegaard supported an incongruity that makes anguish necessary. Now the psyche must work to establish itself, as Sartre recommended. We recognize the fragility of everything human in an incongruous world. Nausea is a natural response to Evolutionary Nature. Ironically, the self is not removed from the center of interpretation, but instead is given the horrendous task trying to authenticate itself, since we have inherited a self that so easily turns to the demonic.

If Plato found it hard to distinguish the universal in the particular, the similar among dissimilars, Darwin has the harder task of sustaining "the perception of dissimilarities in similars" (p.80). Anticipating chaos theory again (physics must follow biology now) deviance, divergence, accidentals are now the materials of sustained change. As with the use of analogy, "the pleasure and power of the form is felt in part because it is 'precarious'" (*Ibid.*). The daredevil, the risk taker, the adventurer are all around us in a Nature that is no longer fixed. The gambler does not defy nature's conservatism but in fact represents and re-experiences the precariousness of our descent. To gamble, to risk, is to mirror nature.

Darwin, like Freud, evidences the impulse "to find a real place in the natural order for older mythological expressions." (*Ibid.*). But note that "the grotesque, the beautiful and the wonderful in the everyday" (p.81) is also a major imaginative theme in Victorian literature. Fact is incontrovertible and yet opens into mystery. Any simple empiricism is thus a distortion of nature and a misreading of the human task. Empiricism holds all the dangers of a dream, since fact and theory converge and must do so (p.82). Thus, Descartes' attempt to escape the dream state is frustrated by the expressions which evolutionary theory demanded. In Darwin's theory 'fact' is identified with what is novel "as much as with what is known" (*Ibid.*). He remarks: "A good observer really means a good theorist." (*Ibid.*). To use analogy is not to fix argument, since "the shifty, revelatory quality of analogy aligns it to magic" (p.84). The relation between unlikes is a living one, one without which we might not even be here to seek harmonies. Hegel discerned much of this, except the fact that no rational dialectic governs our fragile comprehension.

'Approximation' and 'unconscious' become more important terms for Darwin than 'purposiveness'. "Origins can never be fully regained nor rediscovered" (p.88). As Plato had told us in the *Timaeus*, any account of origin can never move beyond the status of a "likely tale" -- but still he advised us to search for the "most likely". The human race cannot be expected to testify to its own origin (quoting Huxley). All thinking, because it is metaphor based, is thus culture-bound (p.90). Theorizing and the making of fiction have much in common. Any present understanding will always be insufficient. We must recognize "a world beyond the compass of our present knowledge" (*Ibid.*), and not just temporarily but permanently. The element of surprise can no more be eliminated from comprehensive scientific theory than from mystery novels, which may help account for the wide appeal of that literary genre.

The Old Testament becomes our Perennial Philosophy/ Science, since major scientific theories "have the function of prophecy" (p.91). Scientists in Darwin's day naturally drew on literary models. The technical, specialized, set-apart nature of much science today has made us often unaware of the imaginative nature of that enterprise. Feyerabend recognized the enterprise "as more closely related to the spirit of poetry than one might think" (as quoted on p 91), so philosophers of science should not be alien to this spirit. Those who do not recognize this, Feyerabend says, are deceived into thinking that they produce a "much grander and more important result, namely, the Truth." (*Ibid.*). The formation of Darwin's plot disallows this.

C. DARWIN'S REBUFF TO EXPERIENCE AND TO COMMON SENSE

Given the scope of history which Darwin's needs in order to account for our present situation and the form of the natural world we see around us, our individual powers of observation are outdistanced. We our dealing, and must deal with, time spans which can never fall under our observation. In order to account for the origin of the world as we observe it, we must refer to a world which no human being could observe. We can reason about our present state and about nature as we see it, but the evolutionary time span is not, and cannot be, co-extensive with our powers of reasoning. True, we can experiment with present structures and their modification, and in the geological record we find evidences of species now not known to us directly. But the picture we must put before our minds is one no eye can presently observe. In closing out the Middle-Ages, Modern thinkers stressed our new-found powers of observation, and they rejected God's transcendence as disruptive. But Darwin forces us to visualize scenes which necessarily transcend both our experience and our common sense.

One does not arrive at Darwin's views on the origins of the species by simple observation and induction. Granted, we find a varied physical, plant, and animal world before us which has unexplained features. But the scene to which we must refer in order to account for their structure is not, and cannot be, put before us (except in fictional presentations). Yahweh taunts Job with the question: Were you there when I set the foundations of the world? Job cannot respond to a power which so transcends his own experience, which divine evolution does, but in like fashion neither can Darwin's reader fully imagine himself or herself present to witness man's descent. Thus, any statement of the theory of evolution cannot be precise in its formulation or be controlled in the implications of its meaning. If Genesis presented truth in mythical form, *The Origin of Species* told a story "no eye hath seen nor ear hath heard."

Darwin offers us an alternative "imaginative history," and it is one which can be elaborated and even partially substantiated by present visible evidence and experimentation. In this slim way, it may now have become a preferred history, a more suggestive *Timaeus* for the modern mind. But still we must ask whether the formation of the account bears a greater resemblance to the work of the creative artist than to that of an experimental scientist. Can Darwin's vast drama be suggested as "the only explanation" for the profusion of species which we observe? He is convinced that every living creature began its existence under a form different from, and simpler than, that which it eventually attained. Thus, we could not witness our own species creation any more than Job could, particularly so since, on Darwin's account, consciousness came relatively late on the scene. Consciousness is not sufficient to account for itself (pace Decartes and

Husserl). Neither introspection nor observation can establish certainty. Much that once was is now gone, never to return.

The origin of life requires death, the absence of whole species. Once upon a time the notion of our descent from a more perfect form of existence seemed to fit our present circumstances. But today we do not even need to believe in religious stories in order to realize that we have fallen or have failed a higher demand, as Camus reported to us in *The Fall*. Yet on the other hand, if our story is really one of ascent from the swamp, if our ancestors are really unknown and invisible to us, that story is a no less a vast and noble drama. In fact, it is more heroic than any descent from a transcendent deity. Still, such a story is also no less 'mythic' in its formation, since it speaks of worlds and times both unseen and vastly different from those immediately before us. Darwin offers us a new creation myth. Yet, when compared with our present state, it is in many ways a more fantastic version than *Genesis*, however more accepted and supportable evolutionary theory has become.

After Darwin (A.D.), we cannot expect our own experience to tell us the full truth about ourselves, nor is common sense adequate to substantiate such an account, since that view assumed that our frame of reference was directly before us. But no human consciousness observed our development, and our own individual death appears as minuscule, given the vast destruction said to have gone before. Present man is reduced to an insignificance such that his ancient trembling before a deity, so much derided recently, seem like a fairly exalted state. If we were created in the image of God, the image of deity which Darwin outlines is of one who operates outside our present comprehension and thus transcends the human species vastly more than *Genesis* once indicated. The postulation of our evolutionary origin has not dispensed with myth. In fact, it requires even greater powers of mythical comprehension to take it all in. And there is no use seeking evidence for the actual existence of a literal Garden of Eden, since Darwinian origins require drama on a far grander scale. Darwinians may still need to deal with a God, but that divinity's original operations lie far beyond our full observation.

The human drama still leads up to us, but evolution's story is of ascent rather than of a fall from original perfection. We are not on the bottom of nature's hierarchy but at its apex. Our world has not degenerated but has actually moved slowly, very slowly, toward a higher state. We can still speak of levels of knowledge, but the procession is upward not downward, however related to natural processes a divinity might be. The death and multiple contradictions we see all about us are not foreign to our original high estate. They actually are merely a minor portion of a vast drama of struggle and death which had to take place that we might live. The drama of life and death which Christianity and other religious set out is not 'unnatural'. It is simply a minor rendering of the struggle life has always had against death in order to promote life.

The Modern World had felt secure with its discovery of necessity, just as Augustine had, and whose influence on Descartes is evident. Luther had not cared for uncertainty any more than Calvin had. But with the evolutionary scheme as Darwin unfolded it, chance re-entered what had long been projected as a deterministic scheme, whose causes could be traced to necessity and thus to certainty. Furthermore, Nature's hyper-productivity, a necessary postulate in an evolutionary story, "authenticated the fantastic", as Gillian Beer puts it (p.193)[3].

Thus, suddenly the Modern scheme is again faced with chance elements and with the irrational. Darwin outlines excessive modes of production that, when contrasted with any religious narrative of our origin, make religious story seem much less fantastic. Surely our present order could have been more simply produced, with less waste and horrendous struggle. Such a picture as Darwin paints seems very little like a neat rationalistic scheme which we might find it easy to accept. Darwin's is a "...demonic theory, emphasizing drive, deviance, and the will to power," Beer claims (p.194). Both Rationalism and Empiricism seem inadequate, and any neat certainty in our understanding is excluded.

We may or may not wish to accept Darwin's story. It may or may not prove to be a powerful hypothesis for science. It may fit with some geological evidence, although nothing could confirm such a theory beyond doubt or revision. But in any case, 'simplicity' and 'ease' do not seem appropriate to postulate as nature's governing principles. God may either be eliminated or radically reconceived, but contemporary theories cannot claim to be confirmed by "immediate experience", by direct evidence, or by what common sense would

---

[3] Darwin's Plot.

dictate. Any deity who does survive Darwin's account of origins must transcend ordinary reason and allow for the play of chance, as well as being one who enjoys the fantastic. We may believe religious stories, but they cannot be ruled out now simply because they're unlikely. Yet neither can they form the basis for unyielding dogma. Nor should authorities be surprised if heresies arise due to the lack of certainty and finality which must govern any religious (or scientific?) account of our origin.

Any God who wishes to create the human order according to Darwin's Plot cannot expect to be believed in absolutely or to be understood fully. Such a divinity can say with certainty: "My ways are not your ways," since it would not occur to us to create ourselves out of so much devastation; it took many centuries before such a scenario for creation could even occur to us as a possibility. It may be mythically true, but its beginning lies lost beyond the limits of our comprehension, since our rational capacities are so little evident in our origins. Theologians had long thought it difficult for us to see things as God saw them, although Spinoza domesticated that possibility for Modern reason, claiming that we could strive to see things "under the aspect of eternity."

Still, how a God could think as Darwin sketches the logic of creation, such a 'Word' could (and perhaps did) come to dwell among us, as the Gospel of John reports. But the full logic of such a procedure is not easily comprehended. Surely the whole order could have been instituted more economically and with less suffering and loss. Darwin's world could never be Leibinz's "best of all possible worlds". At the very least we could conceive of creation as occupying less time and violence, although his evolutionary plot makes current struggle and the vast loss visible all around us seem consistent with our means of creation.

Clutter and profusion reign in Darwin's story, not unity and simplicity as these qualities have usually been attributed to our originating cause. We have not fallen towards multiplicity, as neo-Platonist argued, but have actually emerged from it slowly and tortuously. "In the beginning was chaos," but the voice moving on the deep was, by Darwin's account, slow in producing any recognizable order and left us clear vestiges of our primeval struggle still continued in our advanced nature. As Darwin reports it, our mother earth is not a neat protectoress: It was formed by struggle out of the vast debris of life, not neatly. "Earth mothers," so much admired by Feminists Theologians, should not be seen as merely loving and protecting but as also submerging us in chaos and destruction. Human values were long in evolving; they do not seem to have been original in plotting our emergence. We came hither neither easily nor with any obvious concern about our fragile nature.

Darwin's views on "sexual evolution" require careful consideration. As far as 'truth' is concerned, it is important to see that for him our evolutionary process relies on sexual division. Sex is not minor but major in its role in our evolution. Darwin's written style in itself emphasizes clutter and profusion. On his account studying nature's ways will never lead to a clear idea of God or to a deity who is concerned to "show us the way," since it took so long and involved so much suffering and loss to get us to this point in time. Jesus's life leads to crucifixion, but that is a mild ending, judged by the loss of life which proceeded humanity's arrival on the scene. Since diversity is the medium of development, it becomes much harder to write a clear script for the drama which brought us up to this point. Augustine could not write *The City of God* based on Darwin's plot, since "super abundance and waste are the primary conditions of such survival"(p.126). Creation's opening scenes do not lead us neatly on to God's intended end, as Augustine thought he saw it. And certainly no necessity guided our less than sure advance.

Augustine did everything he could to preserve and to protect what he thought to be the divine 'perfection', and this included binding human free will to God's foreknowledge. Darwinians still see 'perfection' as a guiding quality, although far different from the way Augustine and Calvin conceived of it. "Things through desire of change find constantly their own perfected form," as Beer phrases it. A 'perfect' divinity is not ruled out. It simply requires us to see in God a vast latitude, as one who granted freedom to a somewhat chaotic process, who allows each kind to seek its own form. Evolutionary theory implies a new myth of the past. Instead of the garden at the beginning with clear instructions for our conduct, there was the sea and the swamp. We can have no nostalgia for a lost paradise, since nostalgia is inappropriate for origins like ours. We have 'ascended', but our form of ascent is a new form of flight, although very unlike Adam and Eve's hasty departure from the Garden following their judgment.

Darwin's age talked much of 'primitives' vs. 'advanced' civilizations. Evolution seemed almost to lead up to Eaton. But in fact, our form of flight from the primitive and the barbarous is one which we can never fully leave behind us. This stands in contrast to our long held belief in 'progress', which Darwin seemed to hold to still. But the close of the twentieth century has brought us back more to primitive struggle and waste than to progress, as the century had optimistacally forecast at its beginnings. Darwin knew Malthusian theory of over-population, but he gave it a new twist "by emphasizing the need for super-productivity." (p.130) What Malthus predicted would lead to human catastrophe Darwin did not totally deny, except that, ironically, he saw it as a necessity for our evolution to take place. And 'randomness' becomes central. This leads to his rebuff of 'appearance', a reference so much coveted by some philosophers, and to common sense, so much relied on by many. Our structures appear stable, our actions certain. But behind the whole present scene lies, not Freud's rationally translatable causation, but random mutations.

It cannot be clear why we are here, in spite of Darwin's attempt to reconcile "higher morality" with early centuries of waste and struggle. Nor can our future be certain, if no necessary path brought us to the present. Since diversification is the creative principle, it cannot have been meant for us to hold rigidly to type, not even to our own species. Since there were no fixed forms carried over from our watery origin, flexibility in structure and in conduct is more consistent with our evolution. This stands in contrast to Kant's fixed forms of reason and his universal adherence to moral laws, since nothing fixed governed our progress into the present day. Fixity is not simply artificial, as anarchists believe to be the case. The structures we have produced, or can still produce, were not fixed but came to be established by light years of struggle, and so they can be modified, just as our species has adapted. Much as we may prefer our present state of command and control to our chaotic origins, no 'natural law' allows us to oppose all change. The abyss constantly beacons as we watch violence reappear in 'advanced' societies.

George Eliot felt that "the study of natural sciences goes hand in hand with the culture of the imagination,"(as quoted by Beer, (*Ibid.*)) Imagination roams free and is not restricted to reworking original ideas from sense, as Locke thought. And since our origin came from structures vastly different from those we perceive today, we cannot visualize this from any present experience. Imagination is crucial if the origin of our species is to be understood or described, since it follows from so little that we can see. Rather than a solid ground of fixed bodies, novelists after Darwin pick the sea as the "...necessary element against which to measure the human." It expresses that which is beyond the human and as such is impervious to the commands of language (p.232). The Logos could not have been the sole instrument or facilitator of our creation, as Saint John thought. Jonah and the whale becomes a more significant story than our supposed descent from a divine rational principle, since that origin could not fully dictate the tortuous route of our evolutionary creation.

Darwin creates a central role for 'dread' in human experience, deriving it from biology just as Existentialism took it from introspective psychology. Fear as a primitive emotion survives into the Modern world unchanged. 'Evolution' does nor mean irreversible 'progress' for Darwin. The past is present. Pessimism is often a correct response, but not in some total sense as those who are disappointed feel about the displacement of the Genesis creation story. It is simply because of our sense that the very laws of life that brought us here are themselves flawed, not perfect. Life is attained by struggle, never given to us. Beer quotes Hardy: "...the road to a true philosophy of life seems to lie in humbly recording diverse readings of its phenomenon as they are forced upon us by change and chance"(p.245). Originally 'philosophers' disclaimed that they were 'wise men'. Darwin gives us added reason for such humility, a quality which Spinoza thought Rationalism could -- and should -- remove. Not so now.

There is a new meaning for 'perfection' in Darwin's vocabulary, but it is not "stain free." "... its poignancy derives from the failure of perfection, the unfulfilled, skewed, and distorted."(p.249 Beer) So all was not a garden of Eden to start with, a paradise whose harmony human rebellion destroyed. The process of ascent is both colossal and mysterious. All mystery is not dissolved, as the Modern Age predicted or as the Nietschzian elimination of God hoped to accomplish. Mystery still lies in the very heart of the process of life itself. We cannot be absolutely clear about how we arrived at this point. Beer remarks, overturning Kant's fixed forms: "Our habitual experience is of multiple times which brings with it the incommensurate"(p.251), not a certainty of reference to establish knowledge as Kant postulated. Why? Because in an evolutionary order it is not possible to choose to return to an earlier state. Our present sense of time guarantees us nothing, least of all fixity. Time itself is discontinuous.

As Beer reports, Darwin developed a 'plot', i.e., "that combination of the inexorable and the gratuitous...a strongly surviving belief which pervades both language and the physical world."(p.258) There is a certain faith in man, a certain even 'trust'. Yet ours is not a downward fall but an upward struggle. We work upward from plenitude and diversity, toward a desired unity; we did not fall from it. Ours is "...a unity never quite achieved or allowed, although desired."(p.254) Thus, our human project is to build up Eden, not to restore a fall. Ascent moves in a different direction. Given this as our role, history as we have written or imagined it is not a sufficient guide. Religious advice can be followed, as long as it does not fix deity rigidly in some supposed eternity but sees struggle and loss at the heart of the divine life itself, with uncertainty, novelty, and freedom as the only necessity. We may be "climbing Jacob's ladder," but not as Jacob visualized it. He lived B.D. (Before Darwin). Living as we do in A.D., our perspective is reversed.

CHAPTER II. OBSERVABLE TRUTH

A. UNIVERSALS : USEFUL IN SCIENCE, DISTORTING IN HUMAN NATURE

1. Plato, Darwin and Hegel

Everyone thinks of Plato as the philosopher who was in love with 'universals'. His 'Forms', e.g. Women, Beauty, Good, were timeless and eternal. Each and every thing in the world 'participated' in them and drew its essential qualities from this relationship, not from its particular qualities in time. But in point of fact, the Modern Era is the true advocate of the power of the universal, building as it did on the successful rise of modern science. Obviously, the natural world was at that time, not only being powerfully understood but was yielding to human control as well as to exploration. The universality of science, symbolized in its growing dependence on an expanding mathematics, led many philosophers to assume that now, at last, the vagaries of all past philosophies could be outmoded once and for all.

The social sciences were born. Human nature, which once had been the center of philosophy, now was available to scientific universalization. Freud represents perhaps the most extravagant of these confidences, since for him even the unconscious could be rendered knowable and so tamed. Spinoza saw philosophy as parallel in structure to mathematics, embracing even God in its super-rationalism. By contrast and in retrospect, Plato appears as part mystic, part skeptic, since he did not think 'truth' capable of being given a fixed statement or even of our final comprehension. The 'Good', at the apex of the world of the Forms, transcended Being. His navigator on the captainless ship, as he depicts this scene in the *Republic*, could use his knowledge of the stars unfailingly to guide the ship safely, but the unruly crew will not accept his leadership, even at their own peril. Human nature thus thwarts our use of knowledge to solve even those problems which it might, Plato reports.

Many overlook the increasing complexity which develops in Plato's late dialogues, that is, the way in which networks of relationships come to dominate his view of how understanding must be achieved. Even though he sees the One and the Many as generating an unstable drift toward infinity, Nature as it unfolds before him is fixed in its plan. The frame of the world, that of plant and animal and human form, we may take as given, even when we seek to understand it, i.e., 'explaining' it by constructing myths. Darwin's account of origins would be foreign to Plato, which is why 'evolution' caused such a disruption of existing frames of reference. The motion it requires of our thought, if we are truly to discern our origins, of how we came to be, this frustrated the often assumed notion that 'knowledge' meant fixity not change. Actually, Plato could accommodate non-fixity easier than Aristotle, who stressed the aim of reason as rest; yet both accepted Nature's givenness.

Evolutionary theories have been proposed from the earliest times as one explanation of our origins. But they did not become dominant theories, and none could have approached the complexity Darwin sketched. Similarly, Plato understood the role of 'dialectic' in dialogue and in our progressive understanding. But he could not have envisaged the centrality of motion and time and change as Hegel's new account of 'dialectic' did. Fortunately for the aims of the Modern World, Hegel gave an account suitable for advancing science, telling us how knowledge is formed cumulatively and progressively. This seemed to fit Modern science's understanding of its own progress and its growing power. And if this final comprehension governed human life too, then a complex but still universal understanding of ourselves, of our developing nature, could parallel science. So the Social Sciences were born.

2. The Exemption of Humanity from Science

What we must now decide is why this attractive assumption might not be true, why Modern science stops at the gates of the very ones who develop, control and exploit it, refusing its universalization to their self-understanding. In the first place, that which had been projected to come under our control, to enable the institution of Utopias and the irradication of suffering, refused to obey. Such understanding as the social sciences offered seemed neither universalizable nor capable of instituting radical improvements in human behavior. Democratic societies developed and human rights were proclaimed against tyrannies. But as the Modern drama unfolded, it disclosed little change in the drives which destroyed both men and women and their societies. New societies were proposed, education extended more democratically than before; technologies brought people closer, and communication was vastly speeded.

Still, the record in the daily newspapers, particularly those in which fact appeared uncensored, seemed oddly similar to what had been reported before the Advent of Enlightenment and Science. Somehow the universalization of our knowledge of Nature had failed to capture the psyches of men and women so as to yield us control over them for their reform. True, greater modes of power were developed, thanks to science-spawned technology. But as this higher power was employed, it seemed to create just as much destruction as before, perhaps even more, and not to distinguish between 'good' and 'bad' in its employment. Increased power spawned increased subjugation seemingly with little twinge of conscience -- at least at the time. If a moral law was universal within us, power placed in human hands seemed oblivious to its control. Good and evil, destruction and creativity, still seemed equally balanced, if not opposed, in our actions.

One can say, of course, that the issue is not so much the non-universalizability of human behavior, of our motives and of our character, as the corruption of power, a fact so often noted. The problem is that the 'good', 'courageous', 'admirable' Utopias we were offered were undermined, in spite of the fact that we were said to possess the promised power to recreate ourselves and our societies. "Better worlds" were within our grasp, but we seemed to let them slip out of control. Our problem lies in further improving our techniques, some argued. But this line of happy thought leaves unanswered the

question of why the knowledge and the ideals we possessed seemed no
more powerful against the forces that threaten human happiness than
before. Plato had outlined a utopian Republic but then had outlined the
forces leading to its corruption. In the war to free the human spirit, we
have not outmoded or outdistanced religions, as it once seemed that we
would.

For all that the Modern World has made possible, which is
far beyond the conception of the Ancients, it is hard to argue that we
possess any more power over ourselves for good than for ill. Of course,
where the body is concerned, that is not the case. Medicine has not yet
found the limits on its power to aid human life. 'Behaviorism', the
reduction of the mind to the physiology of the body, is now little
accepted. Psychiatry, based on Freud's scientific optimism, has solved
certain complex cases, but it is not possible to say that it has relieved
our general human misery to any extent, except through the
development of drugs, and that involves mostly our physiological
aspects. The human spirit has refused our attempts to control it, except
by violent repression, which always leads toward eventual destruction.

3. The Non-dualisms Within Nature

Spinoza postulated that all the attributes of Substance or
Nature paralleled each other in their structure. It is hard now to see
why he might have thought that to be so, except for his Rationalism
and his scientific/mathematical optimism. His thesis: Once one aspect
of Nature was understood, the same form of understanding would
apply to all its aspects, a convenient thesis for one seeking simplicity.
More than the fact that mathematics has not developed to be so neat or
so complete as Spinoza thought, the whole status of 'theory' has turned
out differently. That is, we have not witnessed the enlargement of one
theoretical system gradually extended but rather the development of
even new theories, not entirely consistent with but still replacing
former ones.

No one now suggests the "completion" of theory. Its constant
expansion, its revolutions rather than gradual evolutions, do not allow
us to postulate a time for the completion of all theory. This is true for
physical nature even as we have come to bring it within our grasp. If
universals do seem applicable, perhaps there is not a single consistent
set. Plato's world of Forms has turned out to be more complex in its

structure than he could have imagined. Then, as we move to human nature, the failure of any universal theory to offer a greater degree of control or guaranteed improvement seems to render the human future not even subject to the degree of control over Nature's powers that universalizable theories had offered us .

Our human natures do not seem to parallel the structure of physical nature in any helpful way. And if our minds operate using forms of understanding more individual than universal, we can look for little prospect to simplify human understanding and human nature by the use of universal concepts. In fact, we should suspect that universals are more distorting than useful where we ourselves are concerned, that no universal dialectic governs the development of human intelligence and action. Various philosophers throughout history have argued for the necessity of individual assessment, more recently Kierkegaard, Nietzsche and the American Pragmatism. But they are quickly discounted by many who rightly see universals as the only way to develop knowledge powerful enough to induce mass change. The irony in this is that the attempts to reshape whole societies by the adherence to a universal theory have resulted in some of the worst destruction of human beings in our history. Holocausts depend on the supposed applicability of universals to human groups.

Attempts have been made -- "last ditch" efforts in the face of massive shifts in our outlook on the world, we might say -- to hold 'knowledge' to mean only immediate, empirically confirmable statements. This would require the exclusion of psychology and all that is either unseen or might be said to transcend the structures of the natural order. There is, of course, no way to enforce adherence to these restrictions on scientific theory, offered in the hope of 'saving' the universalizability of our understanding. Because of course: (i) the depth of the human spirit which lies beyond sight and control is constantly erupting destructively; and (ii) the only way to be certain that nothing 'transcends' nature would be to transcend it and to be able to report that nothing was "out there" beyond our common empirical reach. But such transcendence kept being suggested by our situation, its lack of completion, its constant disruptions.

Mathematics, of course, presents us with a problem. For if it is powerful and capable of providing a tool to comprehend the structures of Nature, both those immediately visible and those only indirectly knowable, then all that is abstract and non-empirical cannot be unimportant to know. To try to render all mathematics as a construct of the human mind is to leave entirely unexplained why it has any coordination with Nature's structures at all. Kantian "forms of the understanding" are universal. Time and space do seem to characterize most visible objects, although not all of our experiences. However, when it comes to the higher reaches of mathematics, we again approach esoteric knowledge, open only to the few, which cannot be explained as a universal form of all human understanding, since it is not.

Universals, of course, have even lost some of their standing in the physical science, in the sense that no one theoretical structure seems about to capture an absolute hold on all physicists, for instance. Even in biology, powerful as Darwin's suggestions have been, few claim that we have, or can expect to, establish a single theory of evolution guaranteed beyond all future replacement. In fact, the challenge of new theoretical suggestions, ones not previously formulated or accepted, seems to be science's more fruitful form of advance, not the final adoption and expansion of a single theoretical framework held by all. Rigidity in theory appears as a block to scientific advance. This is not quite the individuality of approach that human nature seems to require, but it does argue for a non-finality, a non-fixity in our use of theory -- that no one theory can yield us 'truth' itself.

4. The Absence of Necessity and Certainty

Theologians have long argued for 'necessity' and uncertainty as qualities of God's nature, which were required to support the divine absolute understanding. This secured God's power and control but at the price of ultimately denying human freedom and fixing the outcome of the future. Thus, when the Modern Era of science arrived, the new Promethians were simply proposing, as Nietzsche suggested, that enlightened human beings now seize the expanded forms of understanding and thus control much (not all) that the tradition had reserved for God. Spinoza suggested that we improve our understanding until we come to see things as God does, i.e., under the aspect of eternity. Even Kant's skepticism about our inability to know God or the world directly did not seem to alter our conviction that science could achieve this finality.

We can see "the camel's nose under the tent" in the form of developing democratic theory, in the assertion first of the rights of man, and next those of women, of claims that we are all created equal and endowed with inalienable rights. For if human beings increasingly assert their freedom and right of self-determination, as they are doing, it is hard to see this as the product of necessity. Instead it seems to be based on a growing sense of individualism and of self-determination. If so, this is hard to reconcile with the Early Modern notions of an absolute fixity of nature. Even dialectical systems, whether it is the idealism of Hegel or the materialism of Marx, are not able to account for the way history and peoples have developed outside a single plan. And certainly no monolithic proposal in recent decades has worked out as predicted or with any apparent necessity in its outcome. Human freedom, and our escalating demand for it, destroys every certainty.

Some confusion arises because our thought can in fact let itself be governed by a necessary dialectic. We can design patterns, speeches, theories which operate according to their account. Moreover, this sometimes seems to render human activity, particularly in masses of people understandable, even enlightening. We can arrange all the known philosophies of the world into a scheme of dialectics; we can see human behavior as governed by economics or by class, and more recently by sex. The problem is that, while these theories tend to be intellectually compelling, in fact we have to force groups, individuals, masses into accepting such patterns, often by violence. The volatile qualities of human nature do not fall within any controllable theoretical boundaries except by force. The power needed to gain predictability comes only from an applied external coercion and by the exclusion of any dissonance.

Oddly, necessity seems to be imposed by thought rather than discovered by it, although that distinction is easily overlooked, since no one maintains that the regularity of the physical universe is sustained by our thought. The interposing of human individuals into the physical pattern of predictability is what invalidates the desired parallel. Evidently, we are not easily governed by universal regularities. Although societies and groups do fall into developing and using customs which maintain themselves, we know that these are all subject to change, and also that certain individuals can always "opt out". 'Revolution' is a modern notion, but it rests on the assumption that human beings can modify both their conduct and the structures created to control and to regularize it.

'Anarchy' as a political theory has fascinating implications for our attempt to control/understand human nature and human actions by the application of universals beyond the limits of physiological description. As a political notion, it rejects all social structure as being inherently inhibiting to human freedom and self-determination. And so it is. Most of us accept the need for social/political regularities, even after we have discovered that nothing we name in our governing social patterns needs to be as it is. Possible worlds are paralleled by possible modes of human behavior. The important difference is that the observable universe cannot elect to change itself into another optional form. But human nature, we have discovered, sometimes can, although the shifts or 'advances' are precarious.

The entry of theories of self-determination, of the desirability of individual choice and thus for individual appraisal of all cases which simply do not conform to expectations current at the time, these novelties in human thought and creative effort give us everything distinctive about human life and open its possibilities, when striven for, to all that enhances life. However, all forms of social control, while necessary to keep human life from chaos, cannot be seen as universally governed by any pattern external to human decisions, whether corporate or individual. At any given time most human beings, fortunately, live regular and partially predictable lives. But the independence, the creativity, the volatile potentials in our natures always keep open the possibility of change. It makes universal understanding impossible, but such flexibility and contingency is the source of both the best and the most destructive activity in the human, as opposed to the physical, realm.

5. Description Is Universal, Understanding Individual

The power of language lies in its ability to universalize; appraising the human person depends on grasping what is individual. This opposition is the cause of much confusion. The irony is that we *must* tend to universalize in order to express ourselves at the same time that we *must* separate out the individual if we do not wish to distort. Art, drama, music come closer in their ability to capture individuality.

Direct experience does too, but it defies expression, except for the gifted poet/writer. The poet is the one who can make words bear the burden of individuality while still conveying a sense of a universal applicability. Philosophers have the greatest trouble. They have witnessed the beauty of abstract universalizing. They are entranced by what the power of mathematics can do for them, could they understand all in the world by its use. Yet they sometimes are forced to recognize the enigma of the individual.

The philosopher, every time he or she takes up a pen or speaks, tends to distort the individual perception. Yet at the same time he or she is entranced by the powers of universal description, which work better with flowers and stars than for men and women. The Empiricists knew this and tried to direct us back to immediate perception. Aristotle had told us that the individual is grasped, if at all, by immediate intuition. But the problem with this is that they, the Empiricists, can never agree on the description of any individual perception, just because it is linked to the individual, to additional words, and to the universal. Furthermore, sensory impression, unless extended, confine us to the exterior and so to the superficial qualities of the human being. We miss what is most important, that is, what we need in order to define individuality and to understand it.

Yet sometimes, although we can never grasp all, we must select out and focus on the memorable general aspect of a group if we are to be able to express and to convey it to others. Every description is a stereotype, a partial distortion at best, inaccurate for the whole, achievable only by overlooking non-conforming individuals. And yet it can often still be powerful in its expression just because of the focus which the exclusion of conflicting detail allows. The powerful writer and the graphic artist embody the paradox; they defy the contradiction. Through the insight which makes genius, some detail is singled out which is capable of giving universal expression to what otherwise would seem lost in the particular. The individual, the perhaps unique quality or characteristic, becomes a medium to depict a universal in non-abstract terms. The philosopher, not being poet or novelist, finds this harder to express and so tends either towards individual concreteness as inexpressible or toward unanchored abstraction.

The inescapable problem which keeps us from the final understanding, which we keep being convinced that we can resolve once and for all, is that anyone who comes after the author or the artist can take that combination of words or sounds or artistic expressions, grasp them in their individual meaning -- or in our universalization -- and show that these are not entirely an adequate expression, or even claim them to be a distortion by treating them literally and not symbolically. All Blacks are not ... ; all farmers are not ... ; all students are not ... ; nothing is all anything.

But we are forced into using the loose combination of particularity with a universal quality in order to achieve graphic expression. It is just that this can breed misunderstanding almost as easily as understanding and thus is inherently unstable. Philosophy, if not accepted as a symbolic expression, is either misleading or tends to triviality, even more so than sacred scriptures, since we know that they must be symbolic. 'Fundamentalists' in every field, of course, distort both scripture and philosophy in their hope to reach an unobtainable personal certainty.

B. REVERSING THE FALL, BUILDING UP EDEN

Fecundity, which still is symbolized by 'women', moves upward from chaos toward a partial perfection. Ours is not a fall from unity and an original Eden, but a moving upward from worlds that are nothing like those we now know. As order arises from primeval chaos, women are the symbol of the origin of man, not of his fall away from an originally given perfect state. 'Women' symbolizes his and her and our struggle upward from waste and loss, the fight to survive, to develop toward a level of existence sometimes magnificent but never perfect, never entirely free of loss and strife or the attempt to achieve a precarious stability. Men, like women, do not begin in perfection and fall from or leave it; they have for unimaginable time spans striven and still struggle toward it, often blind to its plan and destructive of nature's resources. The 'fall' is not an Exit from Eden. It represents our attempt, however blindly, to achieve it.

God is not simply the omniscient deity who creates universes and peoples instantaneously as immediately perfect, which we then destroy. 'Deity' is a power still moving throughout our present chaos to bring some order out of waste. It did not create man as lord of nature but works toward a stable Nature and a human nature arising out of impossibly rude conditions never quite left behind. Our problem -- and God's -- is not so much that we have interrupted Nature's perfect order and fallen away from what was originally given to us to enjoy and to control. It is more that today we too often forget our closeness to loss, waste, and primeval struggle. We live oblivious to the fact that our position can only be maintained by a constant struggle to rise above our low beginnings. God works to bring a future out of a loss-filled and often wasteful past, slouching toward an Eden not yet and never quite attained. God is the force of order working through original chaos, and this offers us a different image of our human likeness to divinity vs. of our original naive innocence. For Darwin, innocence and pure quietude would doom us to perish. We could not have survived our origins. Nietzsche was right; he just did not see that "the will to power" is original with us, not a late development to be urged upon us.

Women are not condemned to bear children in painful childbirth because of some mutual sin with an unnatural partner. Rather, she bears the human progeny in threatened loss and physical destruction as the symbol of our origin, of the life of God wrapped in suffering, of how men and women may yet survive and establish order. In occasional present incarnations, God does not descend from eternal perfection into human form. Rather, just as a woman suffers to give birth and to protect her children from destructive powers, God moves through a still-not-yet fully stable order to offer a future to us, as women does in childbirth -- if the offered life is accepted, perfected and enhanced. This world is not -- cannot be -- an inevitable plan ordained in detail in advance. Rather, it represents the attempt to stabilize time and to allow momentary creative bursts. Our model lies not in a past we once inhabited; rather, we imagine God's sufferings, which began not simply with a man hanged on a cross but with primal suffering experienced since before the origin of all species.

Such a God need not be blind or lack both control and power, just as we need not and do not do so when we are at our human best. Yet although such a model of divinity can be symbolized in motherhood, it is at least not as simple as protective love. It should be more as a suffering always to give birth, to stave off the destruction of life. "Motherhood' does not demonstrate a simple caring but rather our struggle for survival. Since we emerged only late on the evolutionary scene and were not on stage in the first act, we can occasionally rise to comprehend nature's plot and God as its author. Yet we never achieve a finished script but rather constantly face a drama unfolding still. Divinity's authorship respects the power of the process of creation, which may yet be brought to fulfillment, but we were not led here by any fixed design. God's power is "supra-natural" in the sense that divinity transcends the evolutionary process in its power, just as at our best we seek in God's image to create art and order.

C. BIBLICAL TRUTH

If we are talking about 'uncertain truth', if we decide that 'truth' is possible but never so as to be incontrovertibly certain, then a good place to test this notion of truth is not with the once supposedly certain physical sciences but with the strange phenomenon of religion, which the Modern Age hoped either to domesticate or to eliminate. Why? Because the religions of the world neither quietly faded away nor allowed themselves to be rendered completely 'scientific', 'natural', or 'tame'. Thus, if 'truth' as the Moderns conceived it was supposed to be beyond any vagueness or uncertainty, a good test case would be to discover how religion escaped that net.

The interesting paradox we encounter is the rise of 'fundamentalism' in most of the major religions, Jewish, Muslim, and Christian. Of course, you might argue that the very attempt to eliminate religion's power led to the backlash which attempted to protect religious doctrine from Modern critical analysis. If the doctrine could be held to without variance, then faith might escape decline. "Biblical truth", of course, means the attempt to use any document or ancient practice, ritual or custom, as the unimpeachable foundation for belief that knows no exception and thus needs no re-interpretation. But what are the aims of religious fundamentalism or its causes, we need to ask, if truth can still be truth but never other than uncertain?

In both philosophical and religious truth, the doctrines, the beliefs, and the founding events tend to be written down, even if they were oral in there beginnings. Thus, we need to ask: Can any thought, doctrine, theory, belief ever be put in written form, no matter what the form, so that the words can convey certain truth to others, particularly to later generations much removed form the originating events? Most know that Zen Buddhism specifically rejects the notion of basing its belief or practice on a written text. On the other hand, other forms of Buddhism use written texts, as do Hinduism and Judaism. Particularly, we know of the way in which the Bible has been made a strict basis of belief in Christian and Muslim communities, "Sola Scriptura", as Luther said. But can words, any words, be counted on to convey such a firm foundation and so to eliminate uncertainty? "People of the Word", we sometimes say we are. But can this 'word' be a written collection of letters, literally?

First, we must face the question of the 'divine' and the caution of the mystics, whether East or West. The Modern Era wanted to literalize all symbols and make 'God' into a "clear and distinct idea", a program which made every mystic's years of strenuous effort seem wasted. On the other hand, mystics of every tradition have contended that the problem, and the reason for his or her struggle is that the divine transcends "the natural", so that normal forms of approach and communication are inadequate if not distorting, even including Wittgenstein's ordinary language or language games. If the basis of any religious tradition or belief transcends our abilities to comprehend it fully (vs. Anselm's 'apprehend', which he did think possible), then supposedly certain 'truth statements' are both inappropriate as well as ultimately impossible. Yet, if this notion is at all correct, how could religious seers ever think or argue otherwise? Of course, we must exclude from this question the charlatan and any who offer religious certainty for ulterior purposes of self-gain.

At this point, we should consider two opposing views. (1) The first one disparages the claim for any final 'truth' in religion, but it holds out Aristotle's hope that in other areas, e.g., physical science, mathematics, there truth might be certainly attainable. (2) The other view point claims to have in fact a greater finality for religious truth, basing this claim for exemption from uncertainty, not on improved Modern methods, but on divine dispensations, appearances, gifts, exceptions made for certain people or groups. What is uncertain is ordinarily made certain by 'grace', allowing the favored a vastly releasing security. Struggle, intensity, devotion may be demanded, but at least in principle certainty is possible, revelation receivable, if only for the anointed. Thus, our questions become: (1) Is it possible for any religious belief which is uncertain scientifically or generally unacceptable to escape third-class citizenship in the land of truth? And

(2) if not accepted universally, can certainty at least by made available to some?

To move ahead with these questions brings us up against the Modern insistence that whatever we gift with the title 'truth' must be universally accessible and similarly received by all. There can be disagreement, but this must be provisional and it should eventually be overcome. Otherwise, any special claim for certainty beyond the generally accessible will be discounted and designated unacceptable in the Post-Enlightenment world. Thus, we have the press of Biblical scholars to try to reduce their inherited documents to a common meaning and acceptability. 'Truth' has always been thought to be found within those documents, but the Modern Era alone thought they had come into possession of the tools needed to understand and to translate what was esoteric into the fully exoteric. Could the universe have been so designed, our question becomes, so that uniform, certain, clear, perception and understanding are not possible? Truth, then, cannot be other than uncertain, although it might still be clearly distinguished from untruth.

How can we hope that the strange world of religious truth will ever enlighten us about the notion of truth in general, particularly about its eventual certainty or uncertainty? Because truth can only be understood finally by looking at the most difficult cases, not by searching out the most simple, in spite of Wittgenstein's suggestion that truth appears in ordinary meanings and languages and the Empiricist love of immediate perception. This assumes that the world we seek to understand is itself simple and so can be simply expressed, if only we find the correct means and approach. But the worlds of physics, mathematics and biochemistry, not to mention astronomy, suggest more and more that the power structures which form and construct universes are anything but ordinary or everyday. In this case, to use simple, clear meanings or forms of understanding is to confine ourselves to the surfaces of our world and of ourselves.

It would be different if we took the approach that religion could offer certain truths, even to the chosen few. But if we claim that no truth, religious or otherwise, can ever shed all uncertainty, then we are claiming no more for religion and no less for the sciences, so recently expanded in their power. Power may result from scientific knowledge; that must be true given medical advance and the atomic bomb. But this need not be claimed to be the result of discovering certain truth, when in fact power has been exercised but found to dwell in uncertain propositions, non-finalizable theories. One can understand and use the power which new theories and experiments provide without claiming a finality for understanding. We once thought understanding and power could only come from clarity and finality in theory, as Spinoza claimed. But by now we know that power is not proportional to the finality or the unimpeachable certainty of any new theoretical approach.

Having eliminated the possibility for finality in the truth contained in religious texts or biblical documents, we still must ask in what sense 'truth' can reside in any written document? 'Epiphany' means the appearance or presence of the divine, or of God, in a natural, historical event or person. This question concerns Jesus, Mohammed, Moses and others in the religious tradition. But at the same moment our concern is with the transmitted, compiled document. Can any such 'divine' appearance, or incarnation ever offer clarity, certainty or finality? Or is our situation such that one is always left amazed but still unable to demonstrate the conclusiveness of the experience or the truth discerned? Can 'truth' be present in written document but never present in a certain or universal form? If the divine and the human always have incommensurabilities, they may join together but never in such a way as to offer finality, conclusiveness -- only unsettling encounters.

So the one claiming to have experienced or perceived life-changing truth in the document he or she studies need not be wrong. He or she just cannot claim universality or finality or final identity with such truth. Universal identity with such experience is ruled out, no matter how compelling the individual response. 'Truth' is there, but not as certain nor as necessarily available. Almost all religious traditions focus on some special individuals or experience as testimony to the power of the truth discovered to reside at that locus or in that person. But this need not be denied if only one uses caution. That what is found cannot, due to the nature of the transcendent, be final or certain, but it may still be a powerful uncertain truth.

If many believe a God or transcendent power communicates or transmits truth in some preserved document, we have to ask about the power of any such person or force to present truth in final form. If this is said to be possible for the divine power to do, our most perplexing question is to ask why this has not been done. In honesty, we must admit that no religious doctrine has attained universal certainty or singularity. The world's religions remain plural and diverse, reducible to no common base. Is a world-creator incapable of presenting truth in infallible form, as Popes are said to do from time to time? Or given our intellectual diversity and complexity -- near chaos, -- may we conclude that documents, persons, events were never 'presented' or incarnated with the intent of providing incontrovertible truth?

One possibility is that divinity understands, as Zen claims, that no text can offer such, that truth is incapable of being presented beyond controversy in such written form. If we do not accept this, we are forced into the notion of a divinity who does not understand what documents or texts can contain and convey, and who thus fumbles in an attempt to present truth conclusively, when obviously one does not credit myths with such conclusiveness. Our other possibility is that any God with whom we deal knows full well that truth cannot be presented in final documentary form and that we would be incapable of accepting it, even so. It is possible that some can be brought to a transcendent level but not that the transcendent can become irreducibly 'natural'.

If you are tempted to dismiss "religious truth" for this reason, as many Moderns did who did not claim to have a formula to reduce it to clarity and certainty, we should ask again first whether "religious truth" is in fact the real paradigm (neither sense experience nor clear and distinct ideas) for the central problem confronting all who seek truth beyond the trivial. 'God' has been thought to be a key concept which is central to all understanding. If this is so, then God's intent (or the problem of a transcendent source) is crucial. If divinity did not or could not intend finality, the non-comprehensibility of God's nature and the transcendent in fact infects all understanding and our hope for conclusiveness.

Aristotle, of course, told us that 'knowledge' differed in different contexts (a concept Wittgenstein translated into a catchy phrase) but one still has to ask the question of significance and importance. And if we have begun to suspect that our most important concepts are precisely the ones that are least capable of finalization, then all truth is cast in a new perspective. If once we thought, like the Empiricists, that using the simple and hopefully obvious events could stabilize knowledge and provide a standard for greater certainty in complex matters (Hume's ideas vs. impressions), if that now seems to be reversed, if the most esoteric and uncertain seem to provide us with the most reliable statements about truth's availability, then we have no reason to exclude any religious truth on the grounds of its uncertainty.

We now can see in what way imagination is more important to truth than fact. But if we first find all religious truth to be not literal or final but always symbolic or suggestive due to its uncertainty, then Biblical truth is neither an inferior form nor can infallibility ever be claimed for it. Its nature and the limitations of our minds do not allow us to do that. We understand the necessity for symbol, image, metaphor, parable -- not as primitive form of expression now to be left behind -- but as necessary if we are to capture and to present a truth so inherently unstable. We see that to claim certainty for truth found in any text misunderstands both truth's volatile nature and our verbal incapacities. The literalist in religion actually demeans the importance of the insight claimed. Nothing ultimately important can be finally phrased.

The irony is that we realize that it is the very uncertainty of truth in Biblical form that causes those involved to claim it as a certainty. This is not merely because the text has moved them profoundly, which there is no reason to doubt. And this also explains why so many who are supposedly certain of their religious insights become in time less certain if not agnostic. It makes us also understand that to claim certainty or definiteness for truth in language or in religious document is to admit that it can have no revelatory power. Documents, biblical texts, stories can reveal truth, but their very revelatory power should convince us that the uncertain truth perceived could never be rendered certain. The very uncertainty of the truth evidences the vitality of the insight contained within it.

D. "THE OATH AGAINST MODERNISM"

After Vatican Council II, in 1966-67, I was invited to Rome to teach for the Benedictine's international college, Sant'Anselmo. I used a monk's cell as my office, and one day walking out into the hall I met a neighbor monk who looked disturbed. I said, "What's the matter?" And he said, "Oh, this morning we all have to go down to the crypt (under the chapel) and take The Oath Against Modernism. Slightly startled, I asked, "What is that?" He then told me that each monk had to swear to oppose 'Modernism' and all that it stood for.

I don't know that oath in detail, and my Benedictine friends tell me it is no longer required, but it was meant to oppose all that 'Modern' stood for. I suspect this meant the rise of science to dominate intellectual thought, the separation of theology from philosophy, and in general all the challenges of Modern life to religious belief.

On reflection, what struck me as odd about this was that, like others who were fighting to preserve ancient beliefs and practices, the Roman Church had in fact fallen into the trap of assuming Modern notions in trying to fight to preserve itself against an onslaught of secular belief. How? Because they in return were assuming the absolute truth of their own position in fighting against the "final-truth-now-achieved" assumption of Modern thought. Against the arrogance that 'belief' was now an outmoded notion, they responded by claiming the same absolute possession of truth, only for their theology and tradition, not for science and Modern philosophy.

Centuries of uncertainty were banished, and the Oath took the strange tack, not of asserting the possibility for uncertainty and thus faith, but of claiming a counter rightness for itself in absolute opposition. The 'Oath' was really meant to be an oath against human arrogance about the certainty and the final possession of truth now achieved in the Modern world. But the perennial theological/religious task is always to translate the 'gospel' in each new age into contemporary terms, into modes of thought which can convey its 'truth' to new generations who begin from different intellectual/cultural starting points. This task can never be done by calling in the storm troops and demanding oaths of loyalty, as the Jesuits once did.

The issue is: Can the old wine be put into new wine skins? Can the religious belief once more be put into effective forms capable of cleansing, changing peoples' lives? 'Salvation' means "giving new life", not trying to hold back the world to old, perhaps even preferable, former times. Nostalgia made into absolute truth is usually self-defeating as a tactic to hold members, whether of a country or of a religion.

Now, at the close of the 20th century, the uncritical assumptions of the Modern World are not so much under challenge in intellectual circles, although they are and should be, but they are falling apart as the world's practice. This does not evidence the change and progress so much assumed to be the result of Modern outlooks? Thus, it is a difference in our outlook today from what most early Modern thinkers predicted that causes us to search for new bases for belief and practice, not any absolutist 'oath' to oppose certainty with another certainty.

The world has turned out such in this century that we need to find truth in uncertain forms, truth none the less, not cynicism or despair. Can our world and its occupants find 'new life' without feeling it can only be based on one exclusive certainty or another? Can we move forward, as the Modern/Enlightenment world desperately wanted us to do, without trying to hold the line against decay and decline simply by turning the clock back or taking refuge in absolutes? Is it possible to find new life in uncertainty?

Chapter III. FAULTS ON THE ROAD TO TRUTH

A. The Good vs. the True

Why is it, one wonders, that all the talented people are not also the 'good' people? In constructing the system that distributes the very considerable talents which appears rarely but brilliantly in human beings, why did God not use the gene system to link these important abilities with all the virtues that the world's religions preach or offer? Instead, we constantly seek to idolize those "stars" in the creative firmament only to find that their artistic, scientific, athletic, etc. talents are not only not linked to the virtues we admire but in fact are often connected to destructive, even self-destructive, traits. The "good people", whom we actually can recognize within the various culture value systems of the world, occasionally possess great talent that can be exploited on the world scene. However, very often, all too often to our dismay, the 'good' are consigned to private lives and to quiet paths, all the while the insidiously self-centered hold the spotlight and reap its benefits.

Is it the case that one needs to recognize faults in oneself, to see the gaps in human nature, to see betrayal and self centerdness in one's own actions and personality, in order to have the world, whether personal or scientific, open to our view, even if this is never more than partial? If we did not feel the surge of power in ourselves to destroy what lies in our way; if we did not recognize in ourselves that pull of attraction when we witness the powerful and the successful walking in front of us; if our own character were not vulnerable to that vast self-centerdness which can destroy, neither could we divine the world's secrets which seem open only to occasional discovery. Once on the stage, on canvas, in print, others can enjoy and appreciate what genius presents. Yet only a character which is itself open to vice can see the world in other than an average way. The path to destruction is often at the same time the avenue to creative discovery. Many are lost along the way, but great are the insights and the discoveries of the few. God or Nature protects some from self-destruction to become saints and seers and literary/scientific/artists.

The link between suffering and creativity/insight is another of the strange connections that characterizes the world into which we are thrown. You would think the design of human nature might have been simpler. Can't we be open to constructive thought without having to be opened to it by suffering? Suffering can destroy, and it does paralyze most whom it touches. It opens creativity only in the few. Suffering does bring forth memorable works and actions, but it is immensely wasteful of human talent in the process. One knows that Blacks have suffered in America, but was that fully necessary in order to produce the Negro spiritual and a handful of amazing writers and athletes? Suffering can never be justified by its beneficial results for the strong few, "the survivors". The majority receive no gifts by its visitation and are left unaccounted for. Can't art and creativity and the perception of truth simply bubble up out of a tranquil world? Evidently not.

Black and white, good and evil, pleasure and vice, all should have been created more distinct and held further apart in our human make-up, we feel. The existence of these odd blends signals no easy understanding of the world's physical or psychic design. In fact, the world's pattern is often so complex, so subject to easy distortion, that it appears as no design at all. "A tale full of sound and fury, signifying nothing" -- Shakespeare was not making it all up. Occasionally in people of impressive and creative insight, it can all fall together into significance and meaning and, we add, produce insight into truth. But such persons are rare, and unfortunately they are not always the people whom we would like to admire or get close to, or who even seem very pleased with themselves -- at least when their public guard is down. We need to wait for some form of revelation to discover truth. The idea that the human world is open to fully rational and scientific explanation is one of the cruelest hopes ever held out to us. The contradictions in the world do not so easily dissolve to our mind's, any mind's, touch.

Can they, then, be dissolved religiously? Yes, perhaps; many have said that this is true in their own experience. But to accept this requires trading one puzzle for another, especially since the variety of the world's religions defies reduction to a rational unity. If the powers and the beauties of the world come together in odd combinations, if insight and creativity originate in often weak and vulnerable people, why was that secret locked away in religious dress, which itself is so often false in its presenters and odd in its claims? Not all the offered religious paths lead us to individual solutions. Many religious routes are themselves much more obscuring than the mysteries of human action which they are designed to solve. Not all practitioners of religion are themselves wise and honorable. "There is a balm in Giliad", as many have testified, but many have also been lost or deceived trying to get to it. "The religious solution" is too often itself "just another trap". Yet it cannot be overlooked; many will continue to try it; and the way must not be blocked, since both the world and ourselves are so odd.

"All is not as it appears in public presentation" -- we must begin with that disorientating proposition. If so, how does one find the 'reality' behind the 'appearances', if these are sometimes so deceptive and so full of contradictions, good-evil, suffering-creativity? If we simply build up our guard against being deceived, construct every defense against being used for another's selfish purpose, if we will not risk ourselves by remaining vulnerable to being "taken in", we have no chance of ever sorting out the contradictions in the world or in people. We may be successful, of course, because a defensive posture will show us how to play the game with minimum loss. But constant openness to what lies out of our control i.e., finding a 'truth' formation, the risk of betrayal, relaxing intellectual pretensions and settling for 'belief' -- that seems to be the only way to individual resolution. And sometimes a religious path can hold one on that course, except that unfortunately the odds of success are not guaranteed.

'Truth' cannot be found in the extremes, although that is an attractive and exciting option for the venturesome. However, neither can it lie in Aristotle's Golden Mean. That is too dull to be true of a powerful, too-often volatile, world. And if 'God' holds the key to truth, it is an odd divinity which wraps its answers in such continued mystery. Yet some have found it there. The only option we have may be to stay open to risk. But not all can or will want to do so. Rugby is not a sport for everyone. Boxing is life-threatening. Gambling can destroy. Our natural instinct -- which we have only Nature to thank for implanting in us -- is to close in upon ourselves and join together to seek security with those who support us. If we agree with Sartre that God can be described as the only being who possess personal security securely, it may not be so odd that such a divinity's creatures seek security so ardently, since they need it so much more. Only a self-actualized divinity has the power to stay open, to be vulnerable constantly. Still, we deify belief into truth and fight to establish it as absolute.

One key to truth cannot work for all, at least where human beings are concerned. There is no need to deny a possible scientific universality. We just have little reason to think it will extend to explain the oddities around and in all of us, Freud notwithstanding. Of course, the top insights in the scientific world are no less esoteric, no less open only to the few. That is, at least they are until, like works of art, they are frozen into marble or into words or formulae. Then the results can be appropriated or, at most, people can appreciate a part and think that gives them final insight. In a world too often dominated, or at least interrupted, by terror and violence and torture, whether physical or otherwise, we have good reason, if we are strong enough, to suspect that opposites lie closely connected. All that glitters is not gold -- not by a long shot. There is no "yellow brick road" to truth. Developing a theory or acquiring a belief is another, and much easier, matter.

B. GOSSIP, RUMOR, PREJUDICE AND TRUTH

Is the academic/intellectual world as free from the first three of the indulgences listed above as it would like to think, so that it can pursue and announce the fourth as its discovery? Not so much as they would like to think or as we might like to hope. The scientific/mathematical world is only marginally, and usually only temporarily, tainted. The theoretical world it has constructed does not profit from deception, and falsity is more easily discovered there than in humanistic, political situations. "The Social Sciences" have never succeeded in their dream to become rigorous 'sciences'. Like Socrates facing the popularity of the Sophists who tailored their teaching to the whim of their customers for pay, we are left to account for why pursuing 'truth' is the less popular avenue.

We might gain some insight into this puzzle by examining a recently popular phrase, "the personal is the political". Certainly any 'person' is connected to wants and desires, and these in turn must be carried into, and acted out in, the political realm, else they fail. Plato recommended the union of the philosopher-king for just that reason. However, if we interpret this phrase to mean that political goals dominate or dictate our every thought and that none can be free from them, we have given up on the philosopher's pursuit of truth and in fact collapsed the philosophical into the "merely political". This voids Plato's hope that the philosopher's pursuit of 'reason' might enlighten, and even improve, the political quest, i.e. to achieve just decisions in human affairs.

One can, even in philosophy, avoid the distorting coloring which political concerns, or worse, gossip, rumor and prejudice, bring into our quest for truth by taking up only questions that are relatively free of such contamination. British Empiricism has often centered on questions involving 'sense impressions', although Empiricism in itself does allow us to consider human passions, as we know from David Hume. Wittgenstein wrote volumes on 'color' near the end of his career, and if we wish truth to be unaffected by gossip, etc., 'color' is about as safe a topic as we can imagine. Plato examined the unclear meanings in our language, but he unfortunately recognized that the most "important" terms, e.g., good, beauty, justice, were subject to the greatest variety of meaning. Thus, they are difficult to analyze just because they are so involved with human emotions and conflict.

Unavoidably 'truth', then, cannot be separated out from the emotional distortion which gossip, etc., brings with it as a result. If so, can we never arrive at truth in the human sphere? To accept this would relegate 'truth' to govern importantly only in the scientific domain and trivially in the human. To approach this crucial question, let us consider just how gossip, rumor, and prejudice do enter into and color human perception. If we can understand both their power and their effect, or at least account for it, can we then discount, if not eliminate, them in order to discern truth? To begin with, we must admit that cold truth is not as exciting as fiction; fact is not as attractive as rumor. Prejudice stirs the emotions.

Why is this? Do we live in a world which is so constructed that there is a natural drift to 'untruth' and an uphill push to discern any truth untainted, plus a tendency to slide back to accept distortion whenever we relax? We must account for the worldwide fact that tabloid, sensationalist, "yellow journalism" is more popular than the "good, gray press". We should in fact be amazed that self-critical, cautious journalism is as financially successful as it sometimes is. We must attribute this to the fact that, buffeted by sensation and prejudice, many human beings are relieved, at least once in a while, to hear a quiet fact. The quest for truth is not as universal as philosophers in their dreams imagine it to be, but neither is it entirely lacking. We must admit that, in a strict sense, it is an esoteric enterprise, one not constantly sought by the masses.

However, to make philosophy into an aristocratic occupation, into the indulgence of an intellectual noble class, this does not do justice to the complexity we face in our daily search. For even among academics, intellectuals, dedicated teachers, one finds an amazing prevalence, a tendency to believe rumor, to accept prejudice. In the history of the world, intellectuals have been identified with many causes, some with totalitarian and terrorist political regimes, even offering racial prejudice and esoteric odysseys. This has so often been true that we cannot define an "intellectual class" in such a way that it is free from prejudice and pursues truth alone. Why, we must ask, is truth in itself not such an attractive goal, and why is prejudice so powerfully appealing to the intellect as well as to the emotions?

Evidently, thought does not come disembodied as long as our emotions have a strong attraction to the sensational.

Consider the association of the 'erotic' with the 'beautiful'. It is true that Plato gave preference to "a little pure white" over much mixed white, which was his symbol that the pure was the beautiful. But in saying this one must take Plato to have been indulging in a slight irony. In the world in which we live, the attraction of violence, as well as the erotic that shades into pornography, have an undeniably wide appeal. In his metaphysics, Plato moved away from making pure 'unity' our intellectual goal, and in the Parmenides he noted that unity and multiplicity are always mixed in degrees; they are never pure or separate. His Forms, too, became involved in complexity and so were not left as simple. We must search for 'truth' but deny that it can be sought free from prejudice, gossip, and rumor. Pure white is not as attractive as some mixtures.

Why? We know the reasons why Plato changed his views on 'unity' and 'multiplicity', but why did he also do so on the purity of the pursuit of truth? Like his altered and softened views on the popularity of the Sophists, whom he thought over-simplified their teaching, if truth is said to be so powerful we must account for why intelligent people all around us are so easily swayed by gossip. First, we must remember that, when someone is told a rumor, no one has 'truth' in front of them so that distortion can easily be discerned. In most cases, "what is the case" is not known. Thus, in our quest for understanding, distortion and prejudice fit our desire to understand. The intellect does not rest content in doubt. Oddly, prejudice puts an end to doubt more easily and decisively than truth. Thus its frequent acceptance.

It is also true that prejudice and rumor play on fear. How? Because even if color spots can be known fully, human beings, in spite of Rationalist and Empiricist attempts, remain essentially unknown in their inner life, and this is always an item of curiosity to us. Thus, if we are curious about someone, our belief in rumor often removes the veil. And why should the rumor not be believed as reported -- if it satisfies? Furthermore, rumor is more emotion producing, at least on the surface, than truth is if known. And when emotion is aroused, there is a strong incitement to believe. This of course is why Rationalist philosophers tried so hard to set aside all emotion and attachment, out of the fear that these would distort reason. And they do. It is just that human beings are not so born that this separation can be made. Our reason is clouded if truth is.

Once we have believed anything we have heard, it is difficult to dislodge that belief. ("He who attacks first has the initial advantage.") We often would rather be partly wrong and have our uncertainty resolved than to admit that we were not as certain as we indicated and that we might have believed something not wholly true. In this way, distortions support themselves, attaching onto what has been called "the will to believe". Sadly, this is not only in regard to religious beliefs, for which William James designed the phrase, but in odd matters of human prejudice which bring us, not closer to God and love, but in fact to hatred and violence. Prejudice and rumor often support feelings of suspicion and hatred that destroys calm.

Plato wanted 'philosophers' to be "lovers of wisdom", not people who claimed to possess truth, which he thought to be impossible. Because his 'Forms' could not be given a final expression in order to render words 'true', this impossibility forces all statements to be less than carriers of final truth. Language cannot bear full truth, since it can never assume completely concrete form. Given this intellectual incapacity, Plato did not himself realize how much more this leaves us open to accept the "half-truth", to be swayed by rumor. We accept a prejudice as correct simply out of our need to be certain and in our refusal to recognize that this is not possible, which would leave us to live in a state of uncertainly. If 'truth' could be made simple, as the Empiricists hoped to make it, or if all our philosophical doubts should be removed as Wittgenstein tried to show, we would be less subject to the distortion of gossip, rumor and prejudice. Distortions are allowed their sway just because truth lies beyond our final grasp, thus frustrating certainty.

Being frail, finite, and human, we do have a natural desire to reach certainty, to achieve finality, and this cannot be removed. Only the valiant few will ever be content to pursue life as a constant pilgrimage, an intense quest which can neither be given up nor completed, although occasionally it is open to insight or to a received revelation. Blocked from simple truth in life's important quest, the majority, including intellectuals, philosophers, writers of all types, join the masses -- not always but more often than we like to think -- in finding rumor and gossip exciting and satisfying. They accept prejudice instead of uncertain truth. They relieve anxiety by artificial conclusions, which, to the distress of 'truth seekers', is far more immediately satisfying than remaining in uncertainty.

C. TRUTH, FACT AND DESCRIPTION

After Darwin (A.D.) we are not allowed the luxury of avoidance by claiming that we do not 'explain' but only 'describe' our world. Nature does not allow such easy understanding, since what we need to know in order to understand we find not before us to be seen, except for certain 'traces' left in nature. Darwin's use (by necessity) of imprecise metaphors to outline his theory, his constant reformulating and shifting terms, results in further imprecision. But at the same time it obviously leads to greater fruitfulness and to the wider use of a provocative theory. Description cannot be provocative; theory can; but not if it is taken as the simple statement of fact.

All this points to the unbridgeable gulf between 'truth' and 'fact'. Facts may be described, but we cannot call anything told to us about the evolution of man to be a 'fact', even if it can be related to certain observable phenomena. Strict empiricism, clear and evident as it may be, cannot then lead to 'truth'. That is something necessarily apart from observation and description, however it may be related. Nor can truth be one thing. This is not because some truths cannot be established; they have been and have been either fruitful and insightful, or else devastating if used as instruments of repression. But obviously 'truth' cannot hold a single form either.

'Belief' now comes into view. Whenever those who hold a 'belief', where even temporary truth cannot be established, reject their lived uncertainty, rigidity necessarily results. Yet they often reverse and claim their belief as an assured truth. They can even become violent when their uncertain basis is challenged, as we know, rather than to become humble as befits simply holding a belief. They devoutly believe something which they should not claim to be a truth and which may even be on the lower end of the scale of possible theories.

'Truth' vs. 'theory' vs. 'belief' -- this is the tension which grips our lives without hope of resolution. Totalitarians have sought to impose intellectual conformity by repression and control. Modern thinkers thought science could bring these three notions into harmony. But the problem with this hope is that 'reason' can never be equivalent to 'truth'. It roams wider by its nature than such fixity. It is attracted to theory and in some cases to simple belief too. But reason, as we know, assimilates all into itself. That is the source of its heralded power. Yet in doing so it transforms what it appropriates, so that reason does not allow us to "know it as it is" (which is fortunate else it would block creativity). So it never finds rest but dwells in restlessness.

Facts and discovery were condensed for Darwin, Beer tells us in *Darwin's Plot* (p.82), so we must admit that discovery is not a matter of "seeing" facts. Facts at times become identified with 'laws'; they were once said to be "God's deeds". In any case, we can now see that facts do not stand for a truth which exists apart from us in pristine isolation. 'Fact' and 'theory' tend to converge. There may be neutral, simple facts, but there are no neutral "important facts", such as those which inspired Darwin. 'Fact' is identified with what is novel in his theory, as much as with what was already known, an interesting indication of "the shifty use of 'fact'". Somewhat ironically, a "good observer", so often praised as impartial, really means a "good theorist".

Kingsley is quoted by Beer: "But who makes truth? Who makes facts? Who, but God?" (on p 81). Darwin, of course, is not anti-theological, but the genius of his insight is to, we might say, "let nature generate itself". Yet the parallel between this outlook and the earlier notion of God creating fact is still startlingly there. Except that now facts do not simply stand there waiting for us to observe them and turn them into theory, perhaps by quantification. Facts do not make truth. The role of the creation is reversed, and we make facts by letting truth stand out in theory formation. Who makes fact? Theory does, since simple facts are meaningless apart from truth as it emerges in theory formation.

'Truth' and 'theory' can never be identical. We do not literally manufacture truth by forming theory. But neither can the two stand apart, nor can it be that facts necessarily lead to truth. That was a romantic assumption of hopeful empiricists. Why not? Because many know the facts but only a few are led to any truth. If facts in themselves led us to truth, the formation of truth would not be so rare, so prized, so much characterized by an esoteric insight not fully open to many who are unqualified to try to grasp it. Truth, oddly, does not seem 'explained' by facts; it is more distant. As Darwin and Freud illustrated as their theory formation advanced, truth perhaps cannot be finally stated.

You must interpret facts or else they are inert. But theory cannot be taken to be truth either, in spite of having just stated its necessity. Theory cannot be truth, because there is no single theory, no final unification of all theory, as Einstein and even Hawking and many others hoped for. Each theory is one way of comprehending facts. Truth, which we appraise and reappraise from time to time, has its usefulness -- or else it blocks us -- by enabling us to solve the problems current for the day. Unfortunately, 'truth' can also disorientate us, because one theory, if taken as truth, rigidifies our perception so that we cannot move to reformulate that theory or use a new theory to greater usefulness. A theory's power fades; what once produced insight becomes a block.

Our problem basically is that we have often thought that the perception, the arrangement of facts, led us to statements that are true, statements corresponding to facts. But this too-simple scheme ignores the necessary intermediary of theory and belief. The mind needs theory to see what is true about the facts of Nature other than what is obviously before us all. All of us do not formulate truth statements equally well, because only a few are skilled at theory formation and its criticism, which alone leads to any insight into Nature. This rare and non-universalizable skill separates us without hope of unity. Since not even all "wise men" agree, there is a further complication in our need for belief.

Could the facts of Nature-as-perceived lead to truth formations, theory might be a neutral intermediary, necessary but not controversial. Since this is not the case, since theories never finally converge and produce one agreed truth statement, as Hegel's dialectic might do, this leaves room for all who choose to adopt beliefs, such as are not counter to every possible fact nor absurd according to all theories, but also never capable of either final confirmation or denial by us on a uniform basis. Truth's refusal to mirror facts in simple statements leaves us in a no-man's-land between enlightening theories and alternative beliefs.

D. MISREPRESENTING TRUTH

As every eager Zen novice knows, the Great Paradox is that unless the seeker is devoted to the goal of enlightenment, unless the effort is intense and sustained, the experience of 'emptiness' is not likely to be attained. Yet, too intense an effort and too hard a concentration on the goal will at the same time defeat achievement, since the focus goes back to the striving self when the intent is to void self-consciousness. Similarly, every contemplative, cloistered Christian monk/nun faces a parallel dilemma: Jesus gave his followers an injunction to relieve suffering, so that single-minded devotion to the aesthetics of the spiritual life ironically turns into a quest to abandon your own suffering, not to relieve that of others. Yet "rushing about in service" is not helpful to the spiritual sufferer, of whom there are many, if the inner life of the server is a "noisy gong and a clanging cymbal".

Thomas Merton's life and pilgrimage is a graphic example of such heroic struggle. He came from "hedonistic frenzy" to the mountain top of contemplation. But his early biographical account drew him such fame that he became a guru for many, making his hermit's life in Kentucky almost impossible[4]. In addition, the classic "monastic disease" is that of a constant urge to change place under the illusion that another environment will allow the perfect resolution. And this drove him constantly to seek new experiences and new people, thus compounding "the contemplative dilemma".

In his illuminating biography of Merton[5], Michael Mott quotes Merton commenting on the controversy which constantly swirled around the interpretation of his literary product: "Of course, when I write anything I write what I think is true. But what is true can be said so badly that it becomes a misrepresentation of the truth" (p.373). If both the Eastern and the Western contemplatives are caught in a dilemma, which is the main "mountain" they must surmount, can it be the case that all the "true" things said to help them (and us) along the way can prove distorting, even disorientating, unless the 'perfect'

---

[4] The Seven Storied Mountain, Harcourt, Brace, New York, 1948
[5] The Seven Mountains of Thomas Merton, Houghton Mifflin, Boston 1984. All page references are to this edition.

form of expression can be found? And if, as Merton suggests, our comforters, like Job's, may in fact be "saying the truth" but saying it so badly that it is a misrepresentation, how is the poor philosophical/spiritual pilgrim to find his/her way?

Other comments made in his account may help us through, if not out of, this labyrinth. "The true danger ... was to confuse the demands of the ego with the demands of the conscience." (p.348). This, of course, is one theme present all the way through Merton's struggle -- and ours. If we do not blatantly admit to self-aggrandizement and pursue it openly insofar as prudence allows, but if like the Prophets one feels the call to some higher vocation, whether in politics, teaching, or religion, then how does -- how can -- one disentangle the ego's demands from what our conscience drives us to? Merton's last "journey to Asia" is a profound mixture of ego saturation and genuine spiritual endeavor and insight. But mixed together do the two distort the truth?

Take the issue of 'emotion', about which both Hegel, Plato, and recent Feminist theory agree: Nothing great in the world is achieved without passion. Noting this need, Merton comments on" ... a restrained emotion of both great serenity and great power" (p.385). However, emotions tend naturally toward the Dionysian, toward the unrestrained, not toward the serene. That is, they usually do if they are strong and unfettered. How can these opposite poles be brought together? Similarly, Mott notes in Merton "... a humility that inspired vitality and confirmed fortitude" (p.385). Spinoza, we know, did not think of humility as a virtue, because it does lower one's energy-striving level, just as Nietzsche thought it made us weak and passive and thus uncreative. Could Merton be right; could humility combine with what seems its opposite, vitality, and actually endorse fortitude, that quality without which little of moment can be achieved?

Yet the writer, philosopher, contemplative who strives to state the truth unavoidably and clearly, or to draw it out of an approach to language (Wittgenstein/Heidegger), faces yet another dilemma. As Mott observes: "What he said was so clear it invited distortion and misunderstanding from those with their minds already made up." (p.370). Even if one already holds contradictions in a creative tension and bends words to express truth eloquently, there is little or no guarantee this will be even noted, let alone recognized. The very opposing tendencies in the human quest outlined above mitigate against the reception of truth by others, even by "truth seekers". The obvious "easy solution" is to deny the contradiction inherent in our quest and to settle on a "solution" that closes the mind to all that is opposed to our assumption, even when that is put before us powerfully.

And that is not the only situation which induces us to misrepresent truth. Mott again observes: "He is ... alienated by the violence of his own enthusiasm and by that very violence tends to produce the same kind of alienation in others ... " (p.380). Who, when he or she has stumbled on to a discovery and is able to give it powerful expression, does not experience a violent emotion. And who, if not totally ego-centered, does not find the strength of the emotion in himself/herself alienating, if one is not intent on self-publicity? Nietzsche alienates many readers, as many existentialist writers do, by their dramatic and exaggerated portrayal of inner emotions. If, then, truth is not always calm but is in fact emotion producing in proportion to its insight, those not so gifted may easily find it alienating, as every actor or playwright knows who reads critical reviews.

And we are also hampered by the special qualities of the 'intellectual'. Such special persons are not always helpful to other non-mind centered seekers, since surely all statement of truth comes as some form of intellectual product, in its broadest sense. "The intellectuals are prone to attack most bitterly," Mott notes, "not those they disagree with most, but those they disagree with least." (p.390). To be attacked is always some form of compliment, even if slightly distorted and painful. It is always better than to be ignored as not being worth attention. But the vehemence of the attack does not help the earnest student of the truth to see the "pearl of great price" which may be buried in all the fuss. The one who is close to our views but more powerful in their expression is the target for envy. Thus emotion certainly clouds our attempts at appraisal too.

Merton's early fame was almost unwitting; he did not plot his success. But as the spotlights caught him up he discovered a wisdom beyond his original insights: He decided that "he was too old to find causes for resentment everywhere." (p.410). This brings up the complications of youth vs. age in representing/ misrepresenting truth. When we are young we may (not must) possess an innocence that allows easy appraisal. But in the struggle of maturity, one becomes more aware of his/her adversaries, particularly if any level of public notice has been achieved. At this point, one is either caught up in the ego-productive battle or, as age grants to Merton, achieves the wisdom to dissolve resentment. This requires, of course, a certain disengagement, which brings us back to the originally postulated dilemmas/contradictions. The new challenge becomes: Can one not withdraw from the struggl to speak and to be heard and yet not be caught in rear-guard protective warfare which deflects our energy from its goal?

Alienation returns in a form more mature than that induced by our originally postulated dilemma: Merton was coming to see the necessity for a certain kind of alienation. Monks and poets were 'marginal men'; both their vision and their integrity depends on realizing and accepting this. "They saw more clearly because they stood apart." (p.413). In an age that laments all 'alienation' and romanticizes any who are 'marginalized', the monk, the poet, or the philosopher needs to remind us of the distance that "a room with a view" can sometimes (not always) provide the soul. The powerful insight of prison literature is notorious, although that fact does not legitimate political or economic repression.

"The poet must avoid routines, positions, responsibilities -- the poet must be a marginal man" (p.478), Merton states with insight, even if this is slightly romantic and a little ego flattering in its dramatic form. Yet the grain of genuine truth present here raises again our question of 'misrepresentation'. How can the poet, any truth seeker, escape the responsibility to experience a 'marginality' that induces reflection and not be caught simply in a covert selfishness, seeking not to toil as other human beings must?

Merton's final Asian journey is in many ways pure ego saturation. Yet at the same time that he enjoys the pent-house at the Oriental Hotel in Bangkok, perhaps the world's finest perk of traveling as a celebrity, his freedom from the monastic routine of the hermit is also insight producing. Is any pure life possible where truth is pursued?

Merton joins the Trappists in a time of the high water mark of religious popularity and stability. And such conditions seem necessary for the monk's pursuit of enlightenment, since one of their vows is for 'stability'. Yet just as his career as a contemplative unfolds, the church and all religious life is caught in the excitement of revolutionary change. The consequence: "The old era had been replaced by an era of freedom which revealed only the immaturity of the free" (p.535). Thus, the ultimate dilemma for anyone who seeks to see the truth and to give it expression without misrepresentation: Authority, discipline, control must be induced as much from outside as from within. Only then can the human spirit find its own freedom of expression, that razor's edge between authority and license.

Chapter IV. PHILOSOPHICAL FASHIONS

A. The Rise and Fall of Intellectual Empires

Philosophers like to feel that they seek to find the truth and to express it. And so we do. Why, then, is there such a passing parade of philosophical theories, each one passionately attached to by its followers as if it were in fact "the truth"? Hegel's brilliance was to suggest that theories develop before our very eyes, their parade governed by a dialectic that leads inevitably toward finality. Philosophers marched to his tune for some time, but now it only seems to be believed by theologians bent on arguing for the ultimate unity of all religions, an event even less likely to happen, given religious history, than the universal agreement of all philosophers. The Modernist thesis, to use doubt only to find certainty, was in some ways more attractive than Hegel's. If certainty could be found in some one perspective, and if it would not involve finding a way to get all of the world's theories compounded into one framework, we could avoid a sort of total philosophical headache.

Of course, the Modernist thesis was built on 'Progress', and there was some reason to believe in this at the dawn of that era. We had progressed in science, medicine, technology. It was, of course, harder to argue that we had also progressed in art or music or culture, although there were still some brave enough to argue that the later the culture the better. Still, philosophy could not be left classically unchanged if human beings could in fact progress to new heights never to return to their origins. Our theories about ourselves and about our knowledge had led inevitably to progress (at least in enlightened cultures), if indeed we had come so far in acquiring knowledge since Adam and Eve made a hasty exit from their garden. Once acceptable theories could be outmoded, could be replaced. There was a choreographed dance, a cumulative dialectical progression of advanced theories replacing all before them, the whole scenario based on an unquestionable scientific progress.

However, the notion of 'progress' has now come under severe question, given the fact that we can see no progress in the way we treat one another, except that this takes place with increasingly sophisticated weapons. Science also proved to be an uncertain foundation for certainty, since the finality we expected to achieve in unified theory did not emerge. Instead, the very leader in abstract theory, physics, showed an appalling tendency toward uncertainty and chaos, with sometimes tinges of mysticism in its aura. True, as philosophers began to speak in mathematics and to use numbers instead of words to express their logic, a precision seemed to emerge of just the kind which the advocates of progress had sought. However, a suspicion haunts this improved version of philosophical thought: that perhaps it reflects a self-contained world, fascinating in its intricacies and subtleties. Yet in the end it may be more an intellectual construct than a sophisticated reflection of either the world's literal structure or of our minds.

More important: If we had discovered non-reversible Progress, why were these Modern theories not able to solve our human problems, as some had projected? The power of the new logic, this near-certainty in thought, should have revolutionized our ways of dealing with one another so that wars ceased and human beings sinned no more. Of course, there did arise Utopian theories, based upon the assumption that now we did in fact hold in our hands the power to reshape ourselves and our societies. Prometheus had to steal fire from the gods; we marched in with an Encyclopedia of Unified Science and dismissed the gods from their long tenure over us. Leaving behind the crude struggle of one perspective against another, utopian construction became "our most important business", and all in the name of the secular ideal of a human salvation instituted by our own hands and our now faultless logic.

So if the world does not today seem governed by Hegel's dialectic, if the notion of 'progress' lies in ruins along with towns and peoples newly devastated, if science has taken back its promise to philosophers to provide them with a basis of certainty which they can express elegantly in mathematics, if the human-cultural scene has all too much taken the appearance of the re-run of a Greek Tragedy, whence philosophy? And more important: What, in consequence, can account for the rapid rise and fall of intellectual empires? Of course, at this point we have to stop and ring the boat drill alarm and ask how many want to abandon ship. We can talk about "the end of philosophy", when in fact what we mean is the end of our interest in trying to formulate answers to the questions which life does not stop pouring on us unceasingly. Or, we can opt for the far-from-novel "way out" of skepticism and claim that there are no answers, when in fact our problem plainly is that there are "answers", just too many of them.

A story is told about Luther's Protestant reliance on the bible, when in fact he had taught a critical non-dependence on scripture in his monastery before his forced exit from the Roman church. Since he had taught a liberal method for the interpretation of scripture, and if scriptures were not the basis of truth and certainty for the Roman church, why did Luther fall back on 'Sola Scriptura' once outside the church? Because he had never intended to leave the authority, the certainty, the majesty of Rome; he needed it. Once out in the intellectual cold, what could replace that basis of certainty and provide an absolute ground for what otherwise would be a matter of uncertain faith? Luther seized on the word of the scriptural text as his basis to ground certain conviction -- an odd choice, to think that words could give such certainty. It was something he would never have accepted while inside a secure and authoritative church.

In the face of philosophy's failure to find a certain base in modern science, which looked so attractive after centuries of going it alone in uncertainty, some philosophers suggested that the solution to "the philosopher's dilemma" (how to escape simply living on with the same old problems that come back to haunt us) was to find certainty, the solution to our problems, the rest which Aristotle sought for, all within the very words of the texts which philosophers had always used. Like the Kabbalists who thought God could speak to them through the words of ritual scripture if they had the right key to locate the message, the proper but strenuous appraisal of the language we use was said to provide a solution to our dilemma, that is, our dashed hopes in the certainty of science and in the promise of Progress. This solution to the philosopher's long standing puzzlement contained a tinge of the skepticism some had already fallen back on, since it seemed to say that what had perplexed philosophers for so long were not really the serious problems we thought them to be. How odd that language had held us prisoner for so long and that we had not recognized this before.

The attractive brilliance of this suggestion, once its subtlety and interpretive method is mastered, is that it in a way restores at least some of our dream of progress. If societies can't progress, if a nation cannot be remade, philosophy could still progress and outmode all its former predecessors. For those who accepted its premise, the thesis seems irrefutable, an impregnable theory. Only one fact remained to haunt those who have, in this new manner, escaped the disillusionment with Modernism. The world outside language not only does not seem to have its problems dissolved as philosophy's puzzles fade away; it seems to grow more chaotic, even violent and destructive. Then, do philosophers solve their own mental problems but no one else's?

How do intellectual empires rise and fall, we ask? Does this involve something like political fortunes? Is it like Boris Yeltsin rising from derision to upstage Mikhail Gorbachov? Does one philosopher merely hold center stage until events swirl around him or her and attention is given to another? Does the Toynbee thesis about the failure of cultures and political empires hold for philosophies? Do challengers arise to threaten what is dominant at any given time, so that their survival depends on the ability of the given popular philosophical view to adapt and to adjust? Will those who remain rigid in their concept of philosophical power fall victim and yield center stage to the next theory, one which is more subtle to the changing times? A little of that must be true. Where philosophy is concerned, the political analogy is more apt than simply one of cultural fashion, such as that which dominates clothes or food or cars. Yet there are 'fashions' in philosophical thought that seem similar to cultural shifts.

One has a sense that ideas are presented as convincing with little more exploration of their basis (the comparison of first principles, 'metaphysics', Aristotle called it) than the one who argues for a vegetarian diet. Surely, however, the astute, quietly reflective philosopher is more given to critical analysis, that philosophical specialty, than simply to allow himself or herself be blown about by the winds of fashion. The reply seems to be that a few (very few) are, but the masses in philosophy are hardly more critical than Marx's uninstructed proletariat. In the first place, everyone wants to get ahead, to get attention, to achieve tenure, and that goal seldom comes by challenging reigning dynasties openly, at least not at first. The Trojan Horse strategy is best; join the party, be perceptive of which views to comment on, but harbor a concealed warrior in your chest to spring a revolutionary thought when the time is right.

True revolutionaries in thought, of course, follow a bolder approach. Perhaps they can do no other. They must teach their unknown public to think in new ways, to develop unused mental muscles. They must develop new forms of discovery, convert others to their style of writing, rather than using modes known to their audience as already in vogue. The situation is not unlike that of the innovator in art or in dance. The new venture will seem not-beautiful; thus, the standards of appraisal must first be overturned , their hammerlock on public sensitivities released in order to allow naive apprehensions. Is the beauty of thought, then, all in the eye of the beholder, as those who would make life simple propose? No, the key to insight, the grasp on new forms of beauty, are in the object, in the new dance movements, in the beautifully crafted word, else those words, those objects, could not inspire us beyond the cartoons we see in newspapers and in life.

One error has been to think that insight is all a matter of proper approach. This could have been believed for a time, because it is true that the right attitude in the beholder, in the reader, is crucial, as Bacon, Kierkegaard, and Wittgenstein argued in different ways. But the penetrating gaze required of us does not create the object; it only (sometimes) allows the object, the words, to reveal to us, to speak to us we say, showing the qualities ingredient in them. It is their author's creative command that allow us to see beauty which was not quite recognized in that form before, to grasp insight and meaning not actually *in* the words but which only comes *through* the words. Earlier forms, styles, had done this for us too, but not in this now novel way. The revolutionary path is not easy. He/she must wait for the world's intellectual, artistic conversion experience to occur.

Why, then, do fashions in thought change, much as they do in dress and in custom? Why not a series of successive, successful, beautiful, insightful classical forms, lying all in a row on the shelves of our minds which we simply use according to our whim? Because the artist, the playwright, the philosopher must communicate. And that requires us to have a particular audience in mind, as well as forming his or her own artistic insight or creative use of words. Thus, for instance, old forms of reference to the sexes are not "all wrong", but one would be insensitive, for example, not to realize that forms of expression have been changed by the feminist challenge to traditional modes of speech. One finds new wine skins for old wines, if you will, since the world does not change at our command as much as some feminists hope.

The author/artist in agony is the one who realizes how hard it is to do something new and how nearly impossible it is to get it appraised in terms that are sensitive to its novelty. A philosopher, for instance, begins as we all must by taking existing, accepted work, or in some cases a classical inheritance, and critically remolding it while recognizing its virtues as insight bearing. But in the process he or she also exposes its flaws, begins to ring changes on its unexplored themes. All this is acceptable, easily recognizable. And the philosopher who does this skillfully, paying attention to the power brokers of thought, will gain recognition, even a professorship. But as he or she begins to move away from that day's standards of appraisal, a sense of loneliness and intellectual isolation will increase. Recognition, the acceptance of new forms of thought, comes largely in retrospect.

One barrier remains: Is the new insight, the new philosophy, really an advance? Is a linear sense of Progress involved? If we answer yes, the understanding of the progression of theories is rendered relatively simple. Will the problems, which have plagued us since our expulsion from the Intellectual's Eden, in some way be solved or disappear? If not, what if the Existentialists are right, that insofar as the Human Situation is concerned science and technology do not avail us much but only increase our potential for destruction? If the minds of all cannot be rendered passive by Freudian analysis, if anxiety is ironically increased rather than lessened by the Modern World, then insofar as philosophies concern our human condition they may yield insight, even perhaps individual mental healing, but they cannot ingrain themselves in intellectual history by outmoding all that has gone before and so establishing themselves with finality.

Consider the situation of religion in the Modern World. Freud and Marx both argued that it had become obsolete, powerful as it had once been. This was because they, and multitudes in the age following them, thought science and the dialectic of thought had brought them not only closer to the truth than others had stood before; it had actually placed in their hands the power to cure not only human ills, even mental ills, but society's ills. The record of the forces unleashed by these challenging theories illuminate a powerful effect. But when the rhetoric dies down and the injured, whether physically or psychologically, are counted, it is hard to feel that the intellectual millennium has arrived. Today one can feel an instinct to pray to God, to any God who will listen to a plea for forgiveness for our massive inhumanity, which is so widespread in spite of our intellectual advance.

Religion involves all kinds of superstitions and popular exploitations of the pious. In that sense it is like any salesman's (or saleswoman's) pitch. Yet it was more the transcendence of God that worried social revolutionaries, since they needed all power to be transferred into their hands. And it was also God's possible transcendence of our rational powers that worried philosophers, since they wanted to understand the world and themselves whole and complete, and to do so without pleading for inspiration from the gods to break down impenetrable barriers, as some Greeks had done. If the intellect had to be master in its own house (now that Freud had rendered the unconscious rational), any God who stood above reason's final articulation would have to abdicate along with the world's other monarchs. True, Rationalist philosophers had claimed 'God' to be an easy, simple, and clear idea present in the minds of all. But the continued terror in the world makes that appear as a dream; it is a divinity which does not help us.

If there are philosophical fashions, if intellectual empires do rise and fall, if God's expulsion was premature and any number of things now seem to transcend our grasp, does theology win in the

ninth inning, return in its robes and with its incense, to befog the clear
philosopher's mind? Not necessarily. Nothing returns to fashion of
necessity, a fact which all must adopt to the exclusion of all finalizing
of philosophical frameworks. It is just that God is no longer
automatically excluded by Progress and religion is no longer
necessarily an archaic power banished by the Enlightenment. True, the
sought for Enlightenment, whether in the East or in the West, is still a
magnificent goal to be recommended to the young by their teachers. It
is just not quite as clearly a search that negates all that went before it
in time.

Seeing things a little differently now, in our disillusionment
over Progress and the unmitigated good of Science, disappointed by
the terror now revealed standing behind the attempts to create Utopias
by force, can we chart the future as our forefathers thought they could
and envisage a cycle of the rise and fall of intellectual fashion? Such a
thesis is too simple, too easy. It overlooks the controversy, the
freedom, the chaos which, we are discovering, keeps all things human
-- and even some things physical -- from falling into the net of our
neat predictions. We return to being observers of the world, intrigued,
even fascinated by events as they unfold, political, artistic,
philosophical, and, once again, religious. Our new sense is one of
philosophical fashions, of how and why intellectual empires rise and
fall. This "new philosophy" still allows us to attempt to control our
own destiny, but it also comes with a sense of surprise if we succeed in
doing so for a time. We are, as Pär Lagerkvist said, a "Guest of
Reality".

A sense of wonder, that fabled source of all philosophy,
creeps back into our self-understanding. We watch the unfolding of the
human drama as a spectacle, no longer as the acting out of a script,
neither of our design nor of God's -- that was Augustine's mistake. We
can open the morning newspaper or the latest scientific journal, not
knowing quite what to expect, but we can find it exciting if dangerous
to be intellectual students of a world scene that is never under any
one's total control. And all the world again becomes a stage and all of
us observant philosophers. Or at least we should all be struggling to
understand the scene before us, without any preconceived notion that
we possess truth, *the* philosophy to end all philosophies.

If some wish to pray about this, they should not be laughed at.
Prayer may be a proper attitude in the face of massive devastation. If

scientists still wish to experiment with maps to explore Nature's depths, since the surfaces have proved illusory as guides, they can offer us ever new insights. Some of these will come shrouded in theories about our power, but always these will be the sense that once powerful theories, like once powerful political monarchs, can be supplanted. Theory is an instrument to apprehension, not truth's final forum. The goddess Truth laughs at the thought that she can be so easily domesticated, even by new atom smashers or super computers. These are the sophisticated toys of genius but not the cathedrals of final truth. Philosophers, then, can continue to enjoin others to "know thyself" and captivate themselves and their students by the sense of wisdom which their theories often generate.

But any sense of finality in theory is gone -- gone with the wind and the anti-bellum South. Empires will continue to rise and fall, as political unions and rock bands form, hold together for "one brief shining hour", then disband and break up, sometimes at what seems like the very pinnacle of their success. "Camelot happens". Perhaps it is success itself that makes the talented artist uneasy. He or she knows it cannot be lasting, that the artistic triumph is a castle built on sand and will shift, if the creator is self-perceptive. So the sensitive, successful artist-philosopher-politician knows how unsteady the base of all philosophic-artistic-political theory is. No profound artist-politician-philosopher ever stays with his or her already acknowledged success, but rather restlessly moves ahead of critics by changing the very insightful form he or she has created.

In retrospect, we see that art historians, political commentators, scholars of the famous philosophies, earn reputations by trying to show that the early stages of a creative mind accumulated to form a smooth development into the later doctrine. Yet all the while anyone close to the anxiety and dread (and their potential destructiveness and unhappiness) of the creative talent knows that it does not all evolve as a seamless plan. One can reject what one has given birth to and start afresh, leaving the critics to lavish praise on what one no longer sees as one's ultimate creative insight. The perfectionist, which every genuine creative talent must be (the "flower people" were not creative, just innocently enjoyable) is hard to live with, constantly making him/herself more unsatisfied with what he or she has produced than any critic could. Having writ, the creative hand moves on. Restlessness is the life of every innovator, and ironically of every imitator too, since they know they lack the very talent they admire -- and criticize.

Theoretical physics has brought a restlessness back into our intellectual life with which we once thought we had dispensed. Political and human destruction has made citizens more restless about forms of government they once thought to be the final product of human struggle and enlightenment. Is democracy not an absolute advance over monarchy, tyranny, and terror? Yes, it can be, when it is made to function and is not torn apart by self-centered factions. But if our philosophical/human situation is as we have discussed, if it is subject to fashion and the rise and fall of intellectual empires, then there is good reason for the return to a sense of restlessness which grips us all and to the loss of any notion of final security in life or in theory. We wake each morning to start at the beginning once again, in the human drama and in our philosophies.

B. TRUTH IN CULTURAL CONTEXT

"Every philosophy has half its truth from times and generations."
W. B. Yeats in *Ideas of Good and Evil* **(p.134)**

'Truth' can be discovered and reported only in cultural contexts. None escapes. Modern science, perhaps followed by mathematics, led us to suspect that truth could be so stated as to escape this cloud. A "cloud" on truth, of course, does not prove that truth does not exist, only that it appears through various filters. Still, as some Feminists have argued, if scientific truth so long thought neutral is in fact at least in some aspects 'gendered', then truth as expressed in science could be less culturally based than other forms but still not escape all local impurities. Furthermore, the immense arguments and serious problems concerning the 'use' of science and the side effects of some of its developments mean that, even if a great many of its factual statements can be considered "nearly neutral", the scientific enterprise in itself cannot be, sophisticated medicine and atomic energy being primary examples. "Medical ethics" leaves no one neutral. Atomic bombs involve vast human complications.

Once again, Darwin may provide a key example for us. We realize how his evolutionary theory was formed and came to dominate, even though suggestions of evolution had long been known. Yet, when we consider the immense implication which his theory contained, we see the whole spectrum of human life and purpose in a changed perspective. Like the origins of the universe and of time itself, these vastly important scientific questions are matters neither open to once-and-for-all settlement nor capable of being ignored. The movement of physics, mathematics, and biology away from simple empirical experimentation, sets scientific 'truth' itself in a new, into an uncertain, context not dissimilar in kind from truth in its various cultural settings. The certainty expected from Modern science, the truth beyond human disputes, fades. Truth is not 'gone'; only its uncertain nature is established.

Given this situation, the final universality of all truth becomes an impossibility, a hope "gone with the wind". Only the creative few escape total restriction to cultural confines; only the strong survive; the majority's succumb and settle for shadows cast on the walls of their cultural caves, to borrow Plato's image of the majority's passive "search for truth". Most are not willing, are not even interested, in struggling up "toward the light". To seek 'light' now, of course, does not mean to appropriate a final truth fixed beyond alteration but to compare cultural contexts (the contemporary version of Aristotle's metaphysics). In doing so one can see what aspects are extractable from one cultural setting and appropriatable by some, perhaps even by all others, or at least by certain numbers in other cultures. For the majority, even in "enlightened" lands, ideas that reign are assumed, enjoyed, argued for without basic question. Cultural metaphysics is a rare, an often mind-breaking enterprise.

Wars are fought, persons offended even knowingly, with little interrogation of the cultural, ideological context which is assumed. Yet such cultural conformity is not accidental. Why? Because only the one who violates his or her cultural context, questions the backdrop into which he or she is born and raised, can discover any truth beyond a given cultural setting. One must not accept at face value what lies not only before us but all around. Only that in a real sense gives one spiritual/mental birth. This is not easy to accomplish but hard, and the rewards denied to "the cultural offender" are considerable. However, "cultural revolutionaries" may make one serious mistake: They slip into feeling that outer conformity, of style and dress and perhaps language, are what must be thrown off. This is possible, but in fact "the subtle cultural revolutionaries", the leaders of the inner, ideological rebellion, are much closer to finding a path to new truth.

What must be done is to draw the comparisons between the various cultural and ideological contexts that we use in order to evaluate and to understand? Those who are rebellious against outer conformity too often get lost by openly exhibiting their challenge and so are not able to perform the necessary intricate comparisons. Those who accept their cultural setting without question and use it only to relax and to enjoy, or to climb the ladder of success by clever conformity, these individuals may be successful or happy in their chosen role. Still, they are prisoners of their time and seldom question it, except as shadows of doubt may drift across their minds. The majority easily, sometimes violently, reject those who do not conform to the norm of their context, even though our unconsciously assumed "cultural stage sets" obviously change from time to time, even from day to day in periods of rapid development. The self-appointed "cultural protectors" combat examples of outer rebellion either by criticism or repression. Inner rebellions are safe as long as their non-conformity is undetected, but the outpouring of their creative work still faces a battle for acceptance.

Given this scene, which holds in general for all cultures, is truth impossible to extract from cultural provincialism? No, the very fact that we can recognize the confines of our cultural settings is evidence that not all are bound by it as total prisoners. The changes we recognize in our own cultural context itself tells us that all has not been and perhaps cannot be as we find it now. The questioning, the inquiring mind (that definition of "the philosophical attitude") begins to search beneath the surface for what can be extracted and possibly "exported". Light shines into our cultural restrictions, and we see at least one universal truth: We recognize the cultural restriction on the truth we seek as well as the battle we face to discover and to extract what can be released to stand free of it.

C. PREJUDICE, DISCRIMINATION AND HIERARCHY

Anarchy is the ultimate revolutionary theory, the logical outcome of democratic struggle extended to its limit.[6] It rightly recognizes that all political/social structures can be and often are used to repress all opposition and to protect privilege. Like Utopian theories, unfortunately, Anarchy often fails to recognize the existence of destructive evil. It is this negative thrust which requires hierarchies to control violence and to recognize the brute fact that we were not all created equal, although we may strive to be. Societies, all enterprises, thrive if talent is located and allowed full expression, a fact which implies that all were not equally born to begin with. Beauty and talent exist and must be recognized. But they are unstable qualities, not uniform but multiple in their manifestations. Once recognized, they tend to entrench themselves -- if they can -- against all competitors, just because they are always under challenge.

Our problems begin with two: (1) There is no single, rigid absolute value structure; instead there are multiple values, many -- not none at all -- given by nature. These can be differently recognized by different peoples at different times. Anthropology illustrates this in its cultural studies . Yet it is totally different to say that we rank values differently than it is to say that none are given in nature, although all values need human recognition to become established; and (2) values, talents, beauties, virtues, all are rightly granted higher rank by our recognition as we establish hierarchies. But immediately they easily tend to become reactionary and to oppose any challenge to their position. Yet all the while, ironically, health and vitality in a society, in a civilization or in any enterprise, rest on allowing new talent constantly to challenge for position. Also, sadly, any privilege not based on strength and talent but on weakness and on an insidious cleverness will move to ingrain itself against any challenge, real or imagined, just because it is afraid that it cannot sustain itself in open comparison.

In recent years, women have made us aware of the vast and limiting aspects of prejudice and discrimination which operate as

---

[6] see <u>Anarchism</u>, Sonn, Richard P., Twayne Publishers, New York. 1992.

natural forces to establish hierarchies. The profound question which haunts all societies, all peoples, is how to allow for hierarchies based on genuine qualities and talents to become established and at the same time to prevent these from immediately closing themselves off from re-evaluation. They either reject all challenge from new talent or become so fearful of power failure, so afraid of not being able to meet a new challenge to their privilege, that one who is established becomes blind to a talent different from one's own. The openness which allows talent to rise and to be recognized turns rapidly into the repression of every new candidate and closes in against all challenge.

Of course, it is difficult to recognize a talent or a beauty that lies outside our current standards of reference. Just as. we were not created democratic by birth but must fight to establish and sustain that spirit, so only a few are able to recognize true talent, virtue, and beauty when these appear. Popularity, whether promoted by the drum beats of TV or by local "talent shows", fixes the public standard or standards. How, then, can the prized few be allowed influence against a vulgar democratic popularity in order to keep open our ability to recognize and to accept new talents without appointing cultural tyrants?

The irony and the difficulty in all this is that the surface qualities used to assert prejudice -- sex, race, lack of physical or mental strength, religion, sexual preference -- are just that, surface features and not the underlying factors. Thus, we can make progress in anti-discrimination laws, in abolishing slavery, in opening societies to wider options, but then prejudice simply moves to take more insidious forms. "Politically correct thinking", so much a focus in the US, has always been with us, because the ultimate challenge to insecure leaders has always been felt to come from those who differ from them ideologically. This is particularly true after a reform or a revolutionary movement fails to achieve its goals, or when it falls into repressive terror. Oddly, when physical, racial characteristics no longer are used to discriminate, ideological purity is often the court of retreat for the prejudiced.

So we must discriminate, seek to form hierarchies according to genuine values and accomplishments, but we should know that the last defense of insecurity is to reject all who do not adhere to a given ideology. The very factors needed to build a creative, memorable society, one that allows the production of works of enduring merit, these same factors cause its decline. This decline begins when those who recognize what has been achieved of real merit turn and then try to force conformity to what itself was once novel and difficult to establish in its own originating time. The transvaluation of values, which Nietzsche recommended, works against the grain of all who enjoy privilege based on once achieved merit, hard won though it probably was.

We must accept the fact that all societies, all races, all religions, all political structures, all individuals, are not equally creative and exemplary, and so are not all deserving of outstanding merit or of being used as models. We must establish rank between cultures and individuals, which requires discriminatory judgment, and we know in advance that this will not, cannot be, agreed upon by all. Much must remain to private not public recognition. Yet such modest recognition can be equally satisfying to one who seeks significance in life that is not necessarily reflected on a public, economic scale. All these evaluations, which we must make for the health and the vitality of a culture, can seldom be seen at the time as clearly justified. What endures is often unsuspected in its own age.

We have to recapture 'discrimination' from its recently negative status in our public vocabulary and distinguish it clearly from 'prejudice'. Hierarchies should be built on sensitive discrimination, on a judgment that is capable of accepting a wide range of values and is able to discern these in as yet undiscovered individuals. Prejudice is quite another matter and involves constructing negative appraisals based purely on one's internal regard. In any field, those who offer public appraisals often indulge in displays of valuation, not in order to open new forms of appreciation but simply to gain recognition and status for themselves. We can never, in the nature of the plurality of values, get fully agreed universal standards. But we can seek to establish those which allow for the new to be developed at the same time that old values are not abandoned totally.

Once again, the Women's Movement offers us insight into these matters and at the same time exposes their difficulty. Women always had value as the producers and protectors of the future of the race or of the society. But they were held to this important but narrow value long after it became evident that they could be released from the all-absorbing burden of motherhood and exhibit new, more diverse, talents. Negroes freed at last from slavery could offer talents other than physical labor. Yet old evaluations, perhaps factual at one time, were used to hold down these challengers to non-change. As one barrier falls, we do not always find the result to be total openness. Other grounds for rejection immediately arise. Black athletes, musicians, singers are beyond denial in their unusual creative talents, but all barriers against individuals do not fall when this is publicly recognized. Society cannot afford a "fast fluidity", it seems.

To gain acceptance for the principle of evaluation based on individual talent alone, whether latent or evident, is still the greatest barrier in the way of human fulfillment. Of course, the ultimate irony is that our problem is not so simple as that each individual knows his or her talents and faces only the problem of gaining recognition from others. For many individuals, their major talents lay unrecognized, unexplored. It is not only the existing society which judges individuals by established standards without regard for innovation. We each begin appraising ourselves by the known standards around us, not by what we might achieve if only we looked further.

If race, sex, and religion have been the most blatant and pervasive objects of prejudice, as the rise of the Women's Movement (or the Civil Rights' movement) makes plain, where obvious grounds are removed, e.g., legal rights established and anti-discrimination laws adopted and enforced, all prejudice does not disappear. It simply moves to less obvious grounds. Modern Feminism is right: Hierarchies still move to defend their privilege, even if this cannot be done on legal or obvious grounds. Every person, male or female, of any race who is denied a recognition or a privilege they feel they have earned can claim this is due to some hidden bias. But millions who comply to the obvious standards of the day are also denied.

Virginia Woolf thought she and other women needed "A Room of One's Own" in order to develop as writers. Yet millions of every race and sex have no such privilege available. Life is too dreary, too all-consuming of their labor, to allow this except for a small number. No society can set up ideal conditions for everyone; only small, highly controlled groups can hope to do this. Thus, conditions much more serious than sex or race hold every group back. It is a rare leader, male or female, who having attained prominence will look backward and aid those who are behind him or her in their climb. In this age we are intently aware of the limitations on the earth's resources. Yet we often fail to see that talent, which lives outside the established routes for its expression, is much more limited in supply than are our natural physical resources.

And so Radical Feminism moves to oppose all hierarchy, all restraint. Yet no society, large or small, religious or lay, can survive and serve its people unless accepted rules of restraint and order, with some ability to establish authority in a hierarchy, are evolved. We need "courts of higher appeal", since local bodies notoriously reflect local mores. But to set up such a higher court of appeal beyond provincialism requires a carefully ordered hierarchy. Ironically, this is just as open to being used for the repression as for the liberation of a rising human spirit. The answer to this fundamental dilemma may be the concept of the "perpetual revolution". We seek to overturn hierarchies which impose intolerable restrictions, ones which not only cut off individual opportunity but work to suppress all non-conforming alternatives. "No taxation without representation", we cry as we continue to dump tea into the harbor.

Revolutions can, of course, turn into terror and wreak destruction, and this they do perhaps more frequently than they initiate a vital society capable of expanding individual opportunity. Revolutions seldom build their new power into a hierarchical structure (of whatever form) such that they allow avenues for constant challenge to the potential abuse of power which any hierarchy possesses. But it is dangerous to romanticize revolutions, since they so easily run amok and simply replace old tyrants with new. Still, any hierarchy which does not find a way to accept constant challenge, to revalidate its right to decision making power, simply sets itself up for failure or for eventual despotic control. We need to question every exiting hierarchy, but not the idea of the basic need to establish one that is responsive to new needs, to undeveloped talent.

'Democracy', we argued at the outset, may offer the best societal means to ensure constant self-criticism for an evolving hierarchy. But there is no single agreed form which political, social democracy must take. Any artery for reform, once unblocked, has an immediate tendency to "silt up" again, after the enthusiasm of the initial liberation passes. No political, social, or cultural democracy can keep itself open for constant total reappraisal. That is exhausting and could paralyze all action. But democracy, where it is practiced in a form not merely to conceal power but to encourage popular critique, may be our best alternative to keep prejudice from reigning simply under a "thousand points of envy". 'Discrimination' has to be practiced and cultivated, else new talent cannot possibly gain recognition. There is, there can be, no perfect system.

Public utterances are no easy indicator of the author/ speaker's mind. How can one "read between the lines" and discover where prejudice really operates, all the while it moves to assume whatever forms are expedient in that hour. As has been recommended, we need to watch action carefully and always see it in contrast to the written/ spoken word. This can neither be done on a mass scale nor in a hurry. Those who are insecure and so avoid open challenge must be skillful in keeping a separation between act and word, using a verbal cover-up. 'Truth' is not easy to find but hard, in physics or in human psychology. Prejudice conceals itself behind acceptable current 'truths'. Can value discriminations, while they build up needed hierarchies, be kept from closing off challenge and so remain open to constant reappraisal?

Chapter V. DISCOVERING TRUTH

A. Fictional Truth

Given the common phrase, "truth is stranger than fiction", could it be 'true' in some cases that "fiction is truer than 'truth'"? How could this be? To understand this, we must first get rid of the notion that 'truth' can mean one thing, that obsessive hope of the Modern World which thought this could be brought about by using one agreed methodology. Aristotle had told us that we must adapt and change our methods, our approaches, for each subject matter and that the 'truth' which results will vary in its certainty. If the Modern World could not overcome this inherent diversity, we must be prepared for 'truth' to cover a wider set of meanings than we might suppose. Works of fiction, novels, poetry, are not 'true' in any literal sense, else they would not demand such exceptional talent to devise. But depending on what they are trying to reveal to us, their symbolic form may offer a truth truer than fact.

Plato commented in the *Timeaus* that his account of the origin of the world was at best a "likely tale". For him, this was partly due to the fact that he did not really believe the world had come into being, into what we now see, from earlier forms. His account of origin was fictive, but he felt it helped us to understand, to sort out, the fundamental components in the world before us and in human life. But if our world has not always been as it is, if it has indeed come into being and developed into its present form and existence as is now commonly believed, then we need to ask in what sense any aspects of our universe, and more importantly of our inner life, can be accounted for visually, literally, and in what ways this can only be done indirectly? How must the cosmologist, the metaphysician, appropriate the novelist's art if he or she wishes to present 'truth' to us in theory?

How can we account for the fact that Hawking's *"A Brief History of Time"* sells more popularly than most novels? The vast majority of his readers could not possibly come abreast of his theoretical physics. Has he, then, managed to use the techniques of fiction to produce insight? This, of course, would not be necessary if every object about which we need to know were visible, open to physical contact, not involved with volatile emotions, as both the Rationalists and the Empiricists hoped would prove possible. Instead, since so much that we need to know or want to know about lies beyond any immediate contact, and since its 'substance' often seems subject to a change or to an uncertainty caused by our own approach (whether in the inner emotional or in the sub-atomic world), imagination must play a key role -- if theory that is useful is to be formed. Was the data Einstein worked with not known to others? Since the visual world is so far from the theoretical world, what allows theory to be formed?

Gillian Beer gave us one account in *Darwin's Plot*. The technique used by novelists, and which changes from era to era and by means of which they construct a plot, bears a close relationship to the way a theory is formed in the prosaic world. Scholarly research shows us how James Joyce used factual, geographical locations in Dublin. But that does not tell us how he is the one who came to write *Ulysses* rather than some other talented Dubliner. Others were familiar with the myths Wagner used for new advances in opera. Other Cambridge physicists knew the data before Hawking. This does not, certainly cannot, mean that any imaginative theory illuminates either theology or physics automatically. But it does illustrate the imaginative, the at first fictive (as Beer says), manner in which a theory that allows for advance is formed.

To the misfortune of "the finalists", that is those who hoped to write definitive theory, "an encyclopedia of unified science", "theories of everything" -- what the role of fiction and imagination in theory formation means is that finality is forever impossible. God becomes the supreme novelist, weaving tales for plots and working toward outcomes that keep the divine hand creative too. Our powers, our minds, our imaginations, only come abreast of this at times. But when they do, great is the illumination therefrom. The traditional metaphor of 'light' as a symbol of truth still holds. But it is now more like a laser-beam light show on a London or a New York stage. The effects are astounding, breathtaking, dramatic. The fixity which Luther and Calvin and Augustine projected onto God we now realize is far too tame a picture for a divinity that can move into the era of a "rock opera" stage finale. Joseph now has "an amazing technicolored dream coat", one more like a stage extravaganza.

Divinity has not lost power in this development but gained. God is allowed a flexibility far beyond Aristotle/Aquinas imagination, since 'imagination' has taken on new and originally unpredictable meanings. The course of history, no less than the interior life of the human race, is as much seen in all forms of art as in any inflexible formula. And as for fixity in mathematics, once 'infinity' no longer held fear for us and the three dimensional world was left behind, the absolute infinity of possible worlds becomes a concept for a non-visual mathematician. Plato, of course, thought mathematics dealt with non-visible but very real objects. However, the range of those often fantastic objects has now moved beyond Plato's 'primitive' imagination. This is one reason why theory now involves fiction in its search for truth.

Theories still need testing, confirmation, perhaps even more so now since no "obvious" criteria pertain. But empirical correspondence or rational clarity is not so much the ultimate test as is imaginative suggestion. This process is not unlike that in art, in drama, in the novel. Much -- a very great deal -- is offered for inspection which is not necessarily worthless; it simply is not inspiring. It seems not to lead beyond itself or its time. Ironically, the critics, the evaluators of the day, are often the worst, or at least are inconsistent, in appraising the new departure. Oddly, theorists in science have become much more used to dealing with a novelty that seems "out of sight" in its time. Does this mean that science abandons empirical testing? "Heavens, no". But it does mean that the physical tests themselves which are to be tried come as much from the imaginative theory as from factual data already known.

Not all that is fictionally constructed can illuminate our inner life or the way this may be connected to outer action, "not by a long shot". We sort through the literature, the novels, the poetry, the art in all forms. Then, after a refining period, a little survives and becomes appreciated widely. Theory formation in the sciences begins no less close to data than the scenes from life which the creative artist uses. The written word in any form is like an art form, not like a fixed object. It can convey truth for us, but it offers literal statements only about trivial questions. Our inner lives, which are our most important aspect, appear to be like cosmologies; they are accessible, not by immediate sight, but only by imaginative flight. This can perhaps be suggested by some flash of insight reflected in our "ordinary language", but then formed into a "Star Wars" script.

B. SURFACE TRUTH

The problem with 'truth' is that only in superficial cases can it be seen on the surface -- which is one meaning of 'superficial'. Philosophers who were anxious to fix truth and to bring it under their control often defined 'truth' in their theories so that it seemed to be a surface phenomenon. If it really is, of course, they must explain why it had for so long not been evident to all. Thus, we have Spinoza's "Improvement of the Understanding", Descartes' "clear and distinct ideas", Hume's 'impressions' vs. 'ideas', even Wittgenstein's analysis of 'ordinary' language (since esoteric language would foil the plot). All were designed to bring truth to the surface, or to explain it as always having been there had we had the right method to approach it properly. 'Method' became philosophy's obsession, since with it lay the key to truth, or so they supposed.

Although there had always been empiricists in philosophy and those who asked whether truth could be located in sense impressions (e.g., Plato and Aristotle), the simplicity of truth, its nearness to us all during these centuries of search, did not arrive in philosophy as a spontaneous thought. New methods in science had achieved much, and so one could assume that philosophy's failure to achieve a similar certainty and power in its theories lay in its long use of "wrong" methods. The problem with this supposition is that, although it has now dominated philosophy for some centuries, just as these philosophies developed toward orthodoxies scientific theory was moving rapidly away from supposing 'method' to be Queen of the sciences. Little in any sophisticated experiment can be seen directly. Fixity and certainty receded; theories failed to stabilize. Science increasingly dealt with a truth not apprehensible on any immediately visible surface.

Freud, although today frequently by-passed, was important to empirically oriented philosophers as a symbol. Since they inevitably dealt with the mind *a la* Descartes, one needed to be sure that the mind's surface could become clear in itself (again Descartes). All were aware that not every thought lay on the surface all the time (e.g., Hume's 'ideas'), but as long as they could be brought to light and did not destroy rationality, surfaces might be rendered clear (*a la* Wittgenstein), language made representative, and truth could be found on identifiable surfaces shared by all. However, Freud opened Pandora's Box, as the Greek's had warned us before. All that he found beneath the mind's surface could not be rendered consistently rationalizable, controllable by the conscious mind, made consistent for all, or accounted for the use of one agreed theory, as he had hoped. Jung foiled Freud's ambitious plot.

Hegel's dialectic, of course, offered an earlier but a more complex agenda for raising truth to the surface. Truth had not been found in a universally agreed form on the surface of the world or of the mind, Hegel argued, because it progressed through history and so was subject to time. However, time's dialectical progress would bring it out, no matter what the suffering and the loss involved. Truth's universality could not have been realized in earlier eras, because it was, it had to, first rise to the surface in far distant lands, in what once were apparently vastly different ways, until time and struggle brought truth to a gradually realizable surface. The outlines of this progress toward truth had become possible to apprehend only in his time. Yet -- praise be to the revelatory power of dialectic -- the comprehensive theory had been grasped and truth's eventual surface could be seen forming in a thousand cultural beginnings.

Yet the clash of ideas, the struggle and even the slaughter perpetrated in their names, has seemed to move us neither toward unity nor even toward a single frame of comprehension, any more than science has become finally unified. Science involves less bloodshed, but the merging of all ideologies, let alone all religions, seems no nearer. Many theoreticians, in philosophy, in theology, in political theory, have not yielded up the golden dream of increased unity and final merger, but the nearness of alien cultures and the speed of interchange which technologies provide has lessened neither the active conflict nor the terror and bloodshed, even if verbally and theoretically it remains unacceptable. If a few philosophers can agree finally to clarify language so that its obscurities are dissolved, public figures can still say one thing and act out, often in secret, another. Lying cannot be detected by examining words alone, as Sissela Bok has pointed out[7].

Since words can be used to deceive, betrayal in human relations cannot be eliminated from conduct by clarifying our speech. More than that, if truth lies not on the surface of language, nor even in much visual posture and overt conduct, then truth will be found on surfaces only in relatively trivial instances, such as color, not in the important and even potentially destructive matters that govern our lives. If we must look beneath most surfaces, in our mind as well as in the world before us, and if we face much intentionally deceptive conduct, 'phenomenology' can no more be a method to bring truth back to the surface than Empiricism can find it there or Rationalism render all apprehensible in a form which all could agree upon.

'The divine', of course, had never been thought to be apprehensible on any surface. God was "greater than can even be conceived", not the greatest object of the mind, Anselm argued. The Empiricists just as much as the Rationalists had to domesticate God if their proposals were to work. Hume dissented from this joint project and reintroduced uncertainty, sometimes wrongly termed as skepticism. As the failure to bring God into full view became recognized, one widely opted alternative was to eliminate God and to announce religion as once having been important but as now obsolete; Freud and Nietzsche and Marx did this in various ways. Religion did decline formally, as well as intellectually and politically, in its public presence. In many cases this was just as well, when our trust in it had been abused or its observance held only to public formalities. Oddly, however, the religious sentiment did not die out in the human soul.

Yet as the program of the Modern World failed to reach universal acceptance and as 'progress' seemed more questionable in its

---

[7] <u>Lying</u>, Vintage Books, New York, 1929.

consequence, science as a leading exponent of the obsolescence of religion changed course dramatically. That which was expected to clarify all former mysteries, that which was retracted from easy public observation, 'truth' became more esoteric rather than exoteric. This reintroduced a sense of the mysterious. Thus, theories could not be propounded as "explanations", as had always been done in the case of God and religious stories, but now must be argued in the frustrating realization that theories which could be grasped and found quite fascinating were not in themselves fully clear, agreed on by all, or felt to be final and beyond destabilization -- powerful as they might be in their practical consequences.

The theories we develop to explain what is not directly visible to us and the language we use to explain these, particularly mathematical expression, these can attain a degree of desirable clarity, challenge the mind, even enlighten it, intrigue it to go further. Yet such theories always remain distinct from, even sometimes slightly at odds with, that which they describe. The world beneath the surface, whether that of atomic or biological structure or of the human mind, remains distinct from any theory. This realm is what Wittgenstein labeled as "the mysterious", that which is important to us and yet is never capable of becoming identical with either our minds or the languages we use. Our discrepancies in language use are neither accidental nor representative of a 'primitive' understanding. Rather they are a profound reflection of our intuitive recognition that that which lies beneath surfaces is beyond final translation, however powerful and beautiful some renderings have been.

God's excommunication is lifted. Although just as we recognize this banishment's end, we know that a degree of mystery returns with it. 'Divinity' has been 'explained' in countless religious stories and theologies. But the mind, the human spirit of the sensitive seer, is neither stopped nor rendered clear by divine confrontation. "The saints come marching in" again - Buddha, Confucius, Jesus, and countless more, each forming a religious following precisely because some have found life's mystery lifted, pain and suffering relieved, human transformation or renewal made possible, by the doctrine followed. But all these avenues do not blend, merge, agree, in spite of the amalgamations worked out on paper and in classrooms. Religions may be immensely helpful to the individual follower, but they tend to divide more than to unite us.

What does the failure to raise truth to, or to reveal it as present on, the surfaces of the world, whether human or physical, tell us about the uncertainty of truth, its possibility but its instability? It tells us that we are wrong to trust surfaces or even to hope to find an approach that will allow any surface to present final truth to us, all the while we search constantly for 'improved' methods. Mathematics has its surface. Philosophical theories have their proposals to achieve an agreed clarity. Scientific theories allow us to grasp or to project an understanding which would not be possible without them and the sophisticated technologies they have made possible. Still 'truth' rises to no universal surface agreed to by all, not even by all specialists, whether philosophical or scientific (although scientists who understand the frailty of their enterprise may be less vociferous in their disagreement with one another than philosophers or political leaders).

We may retreat to such surface truths as seem viable and claim to find a unity or even a certainty possible there, e.g., in color patches or in simple ideas. However, all the while the external world, and the world behind the mind's surface (whether creative or destructive) evidences no such simplicity, nor does it offer any universal agreement. The schizophrenic retreats to another world which he or she has constructed, a restricted arena where peace and unity can reign free. In a sense there is nothing wrong with finding such havens, learning techniques from abnormal psychology about how to cope, as long as we recognize that final truth and significance lies on no surface. The world outside and within continues along its independent ways, producing beauty and horror, excitement and pain, but never final surface truth.

There is one irony involved in our constant search for 'truth' that makes finding it difficult. To most people what is seen on the surface is the most easily believable. Why? It is simply the appeal of the obvious. What is difficult and tortuous -- and perhaps incompleteable -- is made easy. Simplicity appeals over mystery, except to the few indomitable researchers, whether scientific, philosophical or theological. Words can be believed; pictures, descriptions taken for granted. Little was seen by Darwin that others had not seen. Apples had fallen before Newton; sound had been heard in courtyards. Someone had to question the obvious, the conventional, but to do so challenges the security of all but the most adventurous. What is written or spoken can seem to make sense in itself. If we could decide that we do not understand everything, if this conclusion were not so often ignored and surfaces accepted, gossip and rumor would not be so powerful.

'Truth' seems easy to most citizens of the world, and they resist going any deeper. It does not seem worth the pain, the strain. They 'know' their opinion on a subject or about a person. To explore that to which words, whether written or spoken, claim to describe is not easy. Pictures, films may be startling in their impact, yet still tell only part of a story. In movie-making, this is called 'editing'. If properly done, it makes for a more artistic, quality product. In human intercourse "editing out" can come all too close to lying. The line is not bold but thin and hard for us to realize when we have crossed it. How does one stop short of a recounting of the whole history of the world and of the human race, plus its future, if one wants "the truth"? Condensations, extractions, are possible, even necessary for communication. But there is no simple way to tell whether these 'representations' are more true than the "whole story". Probably not, but the alternative of "telling all" is both impossible and incomprehensible.

The other problem, which probably is the most difficult, is that it is possible to take our modes of communication, whether verbal, printed, or mathematical, and to explore or analyze them in themselves. Motion pictures, films, have an internal structure we can explore, else script writers, directors, cameramen, editors would not be so important. Languages all have structures, although probably not a single one. Mathematics offers recognized rules and relationships. Yet these can become unclear, appear so complex or even distorted, that they puzzle the attentive mind. When this happens the inquisitive one explores, seeking clarity, solutions to mental blocks, unraveling confusions. It is possible to analyze language in itself, as Wittgenstein demonstrates. Then internal unclarities can be worked out, "solved". But what relationship do these various mediums of communication bear to 'reality'? Wittgenstein called this relationship "the mystical".

All sciences, all philosophies, all theologies must decide which problems it is their aim to address. These can be taken as comprising "the intellectual world". Yet all the while the physical, mental worlds around them explode and even move out of control. If at any time our forms of intellectual understanding seek to move out of this self-contained intellectual sphere, they must ask: What insight, what bearing do these structures of language, these scientific theories, these religious avenues, have to the world outside the laboratory, the classroom, the church/synagogue gates? Modern scientists ask this question necessarily. Once their theories proved powerful, they saw the chance opening before them to effect, perhaps even to control, the natural world, just as Plato has once wanted to marry the theorizing philosopher to kingly power. With Hegel and Marx philosophy was brought into the same arena. But to play in that league, truth, clarity, insight cannot be thought to lie only internal to theories.

To illustrate our increasing dilemma over 'truth' and its uncertain nature, let us ask a question: "Can the media tell, report, the truth?" This may at first seem like an issue not relevant to science or to philosophy. But it is. It reflects the question of whether, in the condensation of complexity to fit a medium and to appeal to an audience, the   TV camera itself must distort, and whether for widespread appeal one makes what is difficult seem easy to understand -- the old question of Plato's opposition to the 'Sophists' in his day. Does the media even try to present "the truth"? Does it even want to? Editors, space, time limitations, graphic appeal, all make the job of reporting, whether written or on film, extremely difficult. Visual presentations interfere with truth, even though they may seem "closer to reality" than words. Why? Because some events photograph well while others do not. One needs to be "street smart" in his or her deftness of presentation. 'Sensation' enters as an undeniable dimension.

In any attempt to report, personalities get in the way. If this seems not to be the case in philosophy, in science or in religion, we have to ask if that is really so or just less obvious and thus more difficult to detect and to control. How can a story, a film, recreate an event so that it can be fully grasped? The parallel: How can a philosopher, a scientist, put into words, into theoretical formulation, his or her insight into 'reality', into human nature, in a way that makes it effectively transmittable and thus usable? What cannot be grasped can hardly be made fruitful, except as obscurity challenges the solution-seeker to move further, to "try harder". The public has a thirst for excitement and simple statement. One-sidedness is easier for us to deal with.

The media person, the reporter, the film director, the politician, all seek 'sensation', even if they do so in subtle and not blatant forms. How else can attention be attracted? How else can a message be conveyed and not ignored? We need to ask if the philosopher, the theologian, the scientist, the politician are in essentially any different situation? We admit 'truth' to be unstable in all its forms. And this is necessarily so, since it cannot be conveyed in full. It remains uncertain in our grasp of it, since it does not admit to finality or completion in the human mind. Surfaces are easier to deal with for the moment and more satisfying to many, particularly if a little excitement, a little sensation, is involved. The intellectual pioneer must be a performer no less than the celebrated actor or actress, although the context is different and differently handled.

The consequence is that we must beware of all supposed finality, of all value judgments that seem to assume a final authority for themselves. We must admit and accept the ultimate complexity of the world around and within, avoid the lure of simplicity, even though theologians have perhaps wrongly attributed this quality to God and popular lectures have appropriated it as the source of their attraction. But simplicity cannot be a divine attribute. Since the created world so little reflects it, it could not be a primal characteristic of the originator of evolution. The insights we have, the beauties we achieve, the powerful theories we elaborate, whether scientific, philosophical or political, must be preserved, but not as if we think that any one could itself enshrine 'truth'. We know that to be impossible.

Finally, we must reject Aristotle's notion, much borrowed by others, that 'rest', final harmony, 'completion' are achievable human goals or even prime conditions of the divine life. The uncertain nature of 'truth', its fragile containers, does not allow that in our present world, not even when viewed "under the aspect of eternity", which Spinoza recommended. Since God does not see the world or possible universes in this way but rather as generating flux and uncertainty, why should human beings hope to do otherwise, whether one is a genius or merely simple, whether cultured or naive?

C. "FOR NO BEGINNINGS ARE IN THE INTELLECT"

W. B. Yeats, *Ideas of Good and Evil*

If this is true, we follow blind alleys if we try to use the intellect alone to find "the truth" in what is being said or written, since its origin is not in itself. Of course, we have Freud's claim that our ideas are intellectual in origin, just unconscious. But Yeats meant to offer a more radical suggestion. For Freud, origins are in the intellect, although concealed from direct view and confused by continual interference not yet understood, usually caused by traumatic events in our childhood. As these are brought to light and explored, the intellectual 'tangles' are straightened out in analysis, and the hidden workings of our thought are revealed. Beginnings are in the intellect for Freud, but these are often confused, concealed and so are little understood. As a poet, Yeats is more radical than Freud as a medical doctor.

Poetry surely cannot be wholly an affair of the intellect. Its appeal to the reader/listener is as much emotional as intellectual. In subtle ways, its intent surely is to stir, and perhaps to guide, the intellect. If we use poetry as a model, this raises the question of how much of our thought is in fact emotional in its origin, which would explain why poetry's effect can be considered primarily as an appeal to the emotions. The logician, of course, may concede that this is true of poetry but not of philosophy on its critical, rational level. Yet that is too simple an answer, particularly since mathematicians and physicists talk of 'beauty', 'simplicity', and 'elegance', as chief characteristics of, and criteria for, their theories. Thus, to understand thought we need to consider how much of its origins, its beginnings, lie not with the intellect.

Philosophers, of course, have not been unaware of the role of emotion. It is just that for the empirical, rational, scientific Modern era, this aspect was either neglected or categorically rejected. In the *Phaedrus* Plato argued that emotion alone could carry the mind to fruitful vision. The mystics have always recognized its role in their quest. Descartes and Spinoza, true, tried to eliminate emotion from philosophical thought, or to transform its negative effects by a process not unlike what Freud would later develop. Among empiricists, Hume and Hobbes certainly were aware of emotion's role and detailed it carefully, although in both instances they thought its effects needed to be controlled. They did not see it as central to philosophical discovery itself.

Oddly, the supreme rationalist, Hegel, stated that nothing great in the world is accomplished without passion. But like Plato he still saw emotion more as a motive force, a driving power not too different from the way Plato described one part of the soul in the *Republic*. As anti-Hegelian and anti-rationalists, Kierkegaard and Nietzsche (and William James in his own way) felt emotion needed to be acknowledged as having a crucial role in developing philosophical thought. However, what we are considering in Yeats' suggestion is more radical. Not only the process and the motivation of thought, our question is: does the very origin of our intellect, the source of our thought process and its power, really not begin "in the intellect" itself?

If this is to any extent true, which is yet to be worked out, it might explain why Freudian analysis has not had a more widespread effect in straightening out our tangled emotions and thought, and also why Spinoza's attempt to eliminate passion by the intellectual comprehension of causal connections seems not more widely followed. Were the emotions so disconnected from thought, could the intellect stand on its own ground of origin, then science as rationally based, and particularly the social sciences, should have changed the shape of our public life dramatically, as some predicted they eventually would, e.g., Marx. We see the results of science and technology all around us, many aspects of which are amazingly transforming, even if some are difficult in their impact on human life. But alongside this we see no comparable improvement, or even alteration, either in our collective intellectual life or in our conduct of society.

Of course, monarchs have been replaced and democracies instituted, a few with marked success. But most Utopian theories, even including a Marxist form, have not seemed to be applicable -- at least not successfully so -- on a large scale. This need not make us disparage such political, social improvements as have been possible. But the failure of the attempted mass transformation of individuals or societies should make us turn and ask: Is the intellect as autonomous, as self-sufficient and as self-producing, as we once had been led to believe? If poetry should prove to offer a better insight into thought's origin, and if emotion is not subsidiary but in fact originating, the sources of our intellectual thought need radical reinvestigation.

What would it mean to say "no beginnings are in the intellect"? It need not mean that all in our mind is a sea of emotions from which thoughts appear on the surface. Thought and emotion could still be distinct faculties, as Plato thought they were, but the intellect would not move itself. The origins of its movement could lie within emotion. The intellect would not be self-starting or even in control of its power source, although it could develop reflective and self-reflective capacities. But if its origins are not in itself, and if the beginning of all thought is not within the intellect, this has radical implications for the nature of 'truth', particularly for how we discover "what is true" and how we deal with it. The sources for thought's appraisal may not lie with the intellect in a majority of situations. We may not have the power to determine truth from thought itself.

Spinoza knew that 'origins', 'beginnings' were important, but he was sure that these lay within thought, just as Descartes was too, once emotion's distortions were set aside, i.e., understood. However, if the origins of our power, of our creativity, of the driving force of thought itself lie outside the intellect, that fact would mean that the intellect would neither be capable of exploring its own beginnings nor of establishing 'truth' independently, as both Descartes and Spinoza hoped. Of course, some intellectual enterprises, e.g., logic, are self-contained. They may be intellectually founded and so can be explored solely along that avenue. But the philosopher's as well as the vast public's 'intellect', would have no such intellectual origins, and philosophers could claim no exemption.

Of course, if philosophy is willing to confine both its subject matter and its impact to a self-developed intellectual arena, it could still treat the intellect as autonomous. However, since theory of any significance might not itself be solely intellectual in its beginnings, philosophy would have to accept its theoretical sources and inquire into them, a necessary enterprise which Aristotle proposed as 'metaphysics'. But more important: Since only a small amount of thought as it dominates public affairs would be strictly intellectual in its founding, philosophy would have to give up its quest, as recommended by Plato, of trying to unite its analytical skill with kingly powers. Thought and its discovered 'truth' would be ineffectual outside all but strictly self-defined intellectual systems. If philosophy wishes to be effective in our public life, it would have to begin by recognizing thought's origins as being outside the intellect.

If Freud offers one example of the hope to bring all beginnings under the control of the intellect, Marx and Pragmatism are two clear examples of wishing to link philosophical understanding more closely to practical effect. William James (and Wittgenstein) want to judge 'belief' not on intellectual grounds but by its practical effect, not as ideologically evaluated but as demonstrated by its impact on our behavior. Marx is famous for saying that our aim now is not to understand the world but to change it. Given both the dramatic influence of Marxism and its recent demise in many countries, we need to ask: If theory is not self-generated by the intellect, what do its 'beginnings' tell us about both its powers and its limitations?

We realize immediately that a theory can be intellectually compelling but practically destructive, since all depends on its effect on public emotions, their control or their explosion. If, for instance, the origin of much Marxist-Leninist thought in fact lies in hatred and not in a simple rational analysis of history and economics, then its implementation may arouse hatred in its application and allow destructive actions to appear to be consistent with virtuous aims (e.g., the betterment of the poor). This can be done just because the origins of the theory lay, not with the intellect and its insightful analysis of history, but with powerful emotions which the theory's use could easily arouse. Were theory self-originating in the intellect, its effects could be more easily contained and directed.

Still, Freud, Spinoza, and Marx want theory to be used effectively for change, for improvement, for control of the emotional damage we currently see all around us . Yes, but if the beginning of thought, if the motive power for the origins of ideas are as potentially destructive as constructive, and if the test for the difference very unfortunately does not lie with the intellect itself since it is not its own originator, all is different in our relationship to truth. Thus, theory can never be apprised in print, in thought alone, but only as we see its consequences in action. This is particularly so as regards its constructive or destructive effect on human emotions and on individual souls, since therein lie all the 'beginnings' of the intellect, as much for evil as for good in their independence from thought.

personal or scientific, open to our view, even if this is never more than partial? If we did not feel the surge of power in ourselves to destroy what lies in our way; if we did not recognize in ourselves that pull of attraction when we witness the powerful and the successful walking in front of us; if our own character were not vulnerable to that vast self-centeredness which can destroy; neither could we divine the world's secrets which seem open only to occasional discovery. Once on the stage, on canvas, in print others can enjoy and appreciate what genius presents. Yet only a character which is itself open to vice can see the world in other than an average way. The path to destruction is often at the same time the avenue to creative discovery. Many are lost along the way, but greatest the insights and the discoveries of the few. Goal of Nature protects some from self-destruction to become sages and saint and literary/scientific artists.

The link between suffering and creativity/insight is another of the strange connections that characterizes the world into which we are thrown. You would think the design of human nature might have been simpler. Can't we be open to constructive thought without having to be opened to it by suffering? Suffering can destroy, and it does paralyze most whom it touches. It opens creativity only in the few. Suffering does bring forth memorable works and actions, but it is immensely wasteful of human talent in the process. One knows that Blacks have suffered in America, but was that fully necessary in order to produce the Negro spiritual and a handful of amazing writers and athletes? Suffering can never be justified by its beneficial results for the strong few, "the survivors". The majority receive no gifts by its visitation and are left unaccounted for. Can't art and creativity, and the perception of truth simply bubble up out of a tranquil world? Evidently not.

Black and white, good and evil, pleasure and vice, all should have been created more distinct and held further apart in our human make-up, we feel. The existence of these odd blends signals no easy understanding of the world's physical or psychic design. In fact, the world's pattern is often so complex, so subject to easy distortion, that it appears as no design at all. A tale full of sound and fury, signifying nothing" — Shakespeare was not making it all up. Occasionally, in people of impressive and creative insight, it can all fall together into significance and meaning and, we add, produce insight into truth. But such persons are rare, and unfortunately they are not always the people whom we would like to admire or get close to, or who even seem very

Chapter VI. THE WORLD ACCORDING TO YEATS

A. THE DESPOTISM OF FACT

As the Modern Era dawned, 'fact' became important for the Modern optimism, due to its expected human control of nature. It was contrasted, in an always slightly scornful way, with 'belief' so that 'faith' tended to be relegated to the past, as in Freud's *The Future of An Illusion* or Spinoza's *Improvement of the Understanding*. Bacon's name is linked with the insistence on building theory solely on an examination of facts. If so, and if the Modern scientific exploration yielded such power into our hands and so much understanding of our world, is it anti-Enlightenment and a return to "Medieval superstition" for Yeats to urge us to "...this passionate, turbulent reaction against the despotism of fact[8].

Can the poet not see how important a concentration on facts have been to our advance? Or at least, should we confine such outbursts to the world of poetry and art, leaving science and our new philosophy securely fact-oriented? Or could it be that the Modern

---

[8] Yeats, <u>Essays and Introductions</u>, Papermac-Macmilan. London, 1989, p.187.
All page references are to this edition.

concentration on, and celebration of, fact has left something out that is not only important to us but crucial to 'truth'?

Yeats speaks of "...a spontaneous expression of an interior life"(p.192), as we might expect a poet would. As we might also have suspected, his antagonism for Empiricism surfaces when he adds "...and so escape from the weariness of philosophy."(p.193) Of course poets lead us on flights of fancy; we expect them to: "...excess is the vivifying spirit of the finest art."(p.184) But 'excess' is precisely what the Modern approach wanted to get away from and why 'transcendence' and the 'super-natural' were linked with mysticism in a disparaging way as precisely that which we must strive to eliminate. Could modern science prove able to base its whole power and its massive theoretical structure on 'facts', could mathematics be considered as simply a way of presenting facts, we might have entered a new world where facts alone reign. "Long live the new king."

However, at least two things, other than his poetic nature, urge Yeats on to label facts as the new despot in the era of democracy. (1) Science could not base itself solely on fact, important an ingredient as it must be. Rather, its theoretical structures more and more seemed to require imagination of a powerful kind, both for their formulation and for their comprehension. Where Einstein and Relativity Theory, not to mention "black holes" and non-Euclidean geometry, are concerned layman or women find little in their immediate sense experience that corresponds to those concepts. Yeats reports that he "lost the desire of describing outward things"(p.189). And what theoretical physics and cosmological theory describe seems closer to inner imagination than to outward sense impressions. Yeats values words "behind which glimmered a spiritual and passionate mood"(p.190). Listening to contemporary physicists speculate, one does seem closer to the glimmering of a spiritual and a passionate mood than to some immediately confirmable observation.

In a scientific world, legend, myth and story seemed to be "for children only", that is until science fiction began to seem more like a real experience of our cosmology rather than simply a fiction. The Modern World thought we must 'demythologize' and move toward factual accounts and were certain that our history could be detailed as fact. Yet as science moved further away from any immediate fact, Yeats's poetic fire seems closer: "...every new fountain of legends is a new intoxication for the imagination of the world."(p.187) We had wanted to become less enchanted with legend and to move closer to an expected complete factual account of ourselves and of our universe. But as immediate facts receded and scientific imagination seemed not simply inspired but necessary, the intoxication of the imagination became important to scientific formulation. Obsessive attachment to fact became despotic; legend began to appear better able to move us closer to truth than raw fact could.

B. IMAGINATIVE TRUTH

In spite of the Modern Era's hope to reach finality based on a simple description of fact, could Yeats be right that"...the imagination has some way of lighting on the truth that the reason has not."(p.65) The Empiricists just as much as the Rationalists trusted reason as our guide to finality. But as Hume pointed out, had Descartes doubted reason as a guide he should never have escaped doubt. If reason itself cannot escape doubt and so lead us to truth, could it be that imagination, if far from infallible or universal, has a way of lighting on truth that reason does not have? If so, then our hope to bypass uncertainty and achieve universal understanding is in vain. Imagination is individual and uncertain, but at times its creations are not only compelling but revelatory. Are we earth-bound except for the power of imagination, unconfirmable as it often may be?

Descartes sought certainty and thus a permanence for truth through reason's self-analysis. It would cleanse itself of doubt. Instead, Yeats suggests, "...whatever of philosophy has been made poetry is alone permanent."(p.64) If he could be right, poetry is unavoidable as a medium if we seek permanence, odd as that may sound. How could this be true? Because, perhaps, theories based on supposed factual confirmation do not in fact get at the heart of our universe, whether physical or mental. And if imagination alone can visualize what is true of the origin of our worlds, then it is best expressed in poetic phrases. We need to stabilize the world in front of us before we have any hope to comprehend it. And "...the world as imagination sees it as a durable world..."(p.112) not the simple world of fact and sense.

The assumed hope which Modern optimism was based upon was, of course, that nature could be read off clear and direct, once the proper methodological key had been found. If our merely partial success in other cultures and in Western thought before The Enlightenment was due to no fault in nature but to our ineptitude, then could we now adopt tools powerful enough to overcome our heretofore mental weakness nature would yield her secrets without further resistance, including the dark side of our own nature. But Yeats sees nature as not so much uncooperative with our euphoria as unable to conform. "...I always knew that the line of nature is crooked, that, though we describe the canal-beds as straight as we can, the rivers run hither and thither in the wilderness."(p.5) The poet is on to chaos theory and has his own version of an uncertainty principle. Imagination is the source of individual insight and enlightenment, but it also tends to imagine the world as fixed when it is not.

But even more than Nature itself, it is human nature that foils the plot, which is why Freud's mistaken certainty is so crucial to our revised self-image today. Yeats announced his guiding doctrines of how truth can be approached and sometimes even partially grasped: (1). "That the borders of our mind are ever shifting... (2) That the borders of our memories are ever shifting [pace Hegel], and that our memories are part of a great memory... [Jung vindicated] (3) That this great mind and great memory can be evoked by symbolism." (p.88) Spinoza and Leibniz had thought that the Modern Rationalist could see the world as God eternally sees it. Yet ironically, Yeats reports, it cannot be evoked or described directly but only grasped by symbols. Mathematics does not hold a mirror to the world but rather only offers us sometimes powerful symbols.

Yeats as we know was attracted to his fellow poet across the Irish Sea, Blake. What key did he find there that fitted the World According to Yeats? "... [Blake] spoke confusedly and obscurely because he spoke of things for whose speaking he could find no models in the world about him..."(p.111) Poetry is not, then, a life only for dreamers in their romantic modes. It in fact reflects the world it apprehends, a real world, a world ever so important to us always, but not a world which the facts to be seen about us can represent clearly. "The fault, dear Brutus, is not that we are underlings now released to become giants, but that the worlds (and they are multiple and sometimes discordant) with which we must deal are themselves 'out of joint'", to borrow from Shakespeare. Out instruments of understanding can be shown to reflect internal clarity and precision, but in doing so they reflect themselves more than our world.

It is crucial to the Modern hope that Descartes thought 'God' was mankind's most universal clear and distinct idea. For if God must be approached in any other way, or if divinity is creative in ways not always literally expressible, then our computers may not reflect all of reality, save when chaos appears on the screen from time to time. "...Imagination was the first emanation of divinity [not noûs], 'the body of God"..." (p.111) Yeats sees Blake as reporting: In the beginning there was not the Word but the imaginative play of a mind of power beyond our limits. If so, our Rationalism operates within boundaries and restrictions which do not allow it to reflect the entire set of worlds with which we must deal. Flickering as its flame is, we neglect the guidance of imagination under the threat of losing sight of God -- which we have often done.

What was Blake's accomplishment? Yeats reports: "...he had overcome the merely reasoning and sensual portions of the mind..."(p.118) This is not what the Rationalists or the Empiricist wish to hear, since for them our success in overcoming our limited past understanding must lie in the power of reasoning and in the adequacy of Empiricism as a descriptive guide. Early modern science equally took this as a first premise, its unexamined metaphysics. Stratospheric science, cosmological explorers and mathematics, as they reach beyond common sense have left this early optimism behind, sometimes without realizing it. But if the "merely reasoning" and "sensual portions" of the mind must be overcome and not slavishly followed on to some multicultural universal agreement, then our imagination returns as the sometimes quixotic reed upon which our insights and stabilities momentarily depend for their exposition.

We had thought the new path to ultimate success lay in simplicity and clarity and directness. Instead, Yeats informs us, "the roadway of excess leads to the palace of wisdom"(p.123) Dionysian frenzy is unnerving, even sometimes disorienting. But it is not, perhaps unfortunately, just the artist's self-indulgent fashion but the narrow road, "the razor's edge", which we must follow if we would reach the mote around wisdom's castle. God, then, could not be seen in nature's design, particularly not as evolutionary theory portrays its rise from life's almost incomprehensible struggle to achieve human form. "No worthy symbol of God existed but the inner world..."(p.133), but we know that to be the source both of our genius and of our madness, our creativity as well as our never-ending self-destruction.

Did early modern science not so much reflect 'Nature' in its attractive theories as create a new 'Nature' after its dreams? Was its vaunted clarity self-imposed and not recognized until chaos began to flicker on computer screens? The front pages of daily newspapers did not cease to report man's inhumanity to man -- and to woman. Darwin's world was a world of excess and of destruction, not of neatness or finality. It was not necessarily a world without God, but simply of a God with the passion of Yahweh and even the fierce eroticism of the Hindu pantheon. Science depended for its success on a full rationalism reflected in the world, Christianity on a universal love, not simply in particular instances. God faded from view as much because we had misconceived divinity as because divinity had died. The path of excess (Darwin's way) and continued human cruelty could still be fitted to a world of love, but not without abandoning a romantically simple view of Nature.

God "... dwells in the freedom of imagination" (p.138), Yeats informs us. Divinity had not left us; only the God had left us whom Nietzsche found incompatible with the world-wide struggle of our wills. We had wanted keys to unlock Nature's powers in a full and final disclosure. But if Yeats is right and the only adequate medium to express truth is symbol, then finality is unrealizable, since "...no symbol tells all its meaning to any generation" (p.148). The excitement is that each new generation can see new things in old symbols, new riches of insight in old theories. But the price we pay for our continual discovery is the loss of finality, since symbols by their nature conceal as well as disclose. Despite shouts from excited audiences, symbols never "take it all off" to disclose Nature nude. They cannot.

Following Aristotle, most of Western thought had taken rest and completion to represent 'perfection' and as that which our thought must seek to imitate. But Yeats tells us that "...symbols are the only things free enough from all bonds to speak of perfection."(p.148) If so, we have sought the perfection of our understanding in the wrong location. Of course, Hegel agreed partially with Yeats; truth was best expressed in motion. But Hegel thought perfection followed an outlined movement in its progress toward completion. Restriction in order to finalize boundaries was still the goal. All that differed was

Hegel's new approach through circumscribed time and organized motion. Now Yeats adds the crucial rising theme: "freedom from bonds." He has not yet preached anarchy, but at least perfection no longer lies in confinement.

Of course, if we do not advocate intellectual anarchy, as Nietzsche at times seemed to do, we must find a logos somewhere, a law to guide our discovery. Yeats replies: This lies in art. "... The laws of art, which are the true laws of the world, can alone bind the imagination..."(p.113) If true, this has startling implications. Instead of art as decoration and as unrelated to the scientific enterprise, it turns out to be key to all discovery. Hegel again moved part way down the path away from an Empiricism of sense impressions and a Rationalism of unwavering clarity by seeing the spirit of an age expressed in its art. But this movement was an outward manifestation of an inner rationally controlled dialectic. It was not, as Yeats would propose, the very key to a hidden world, accessible only to an active imagination. The consummate artist opens the inner world to view, at least from time to time and at his or her artistic best, but the artist is controlled by no dialectical movement.

Are there then no facts at all? Is all science and Modern Philosophy the result of artistic imagination? This is not at all what Yeats wants to suggest or what is the case. But as science in its theory moves further away from any possible immediate factual confirmation, the very construction of any insightful, advancing theory that yields novelty in our approach must be inspired by the same process that produces fine art. Yet why suggest even this role for artistic imagination, if the natural world is the product of factual design? Because we begin to suspect, as Yeats report and as our insights into nature's fantastic depths beyond directly observable fact increasingly suggest, since the form of Nature itself evolved. What we now explore had no original pre-established design, thus no pre-established harmony, pace Leibniz. As our imagination is challenged at every turn by scientific discovery which makes what formerly were thought to be 'facts' seem constantly new, so the laws of the world were themselves imaginatively formed. We do well to study the "laws of art" for insights from that amazing field and to learn the role of imagination in the way theories are formed so that they open our human and physical world to esoteric insight.

We deal, thus, not with fixed, obvious facts but with increasing subtleties of Nature and human Nature, "...the subtleties that have a new meaning everyday," as Yeats puts it (p.164). The facts of our observable world are still there, sometimes obviously and even painfully there. But their understanding requires an equal subtlety of mind on our part, which is not fixed as a universal approach in us all, most unfortunately not. Human beings appear fixed at times in what we might call " a blessed stability of culture". But we know that no crass approach yields a powerful understanding of the springs of our behavior, no more so than it would to the atom's life, else sense experience would makes Shakespeares of us all. Facts are there, still there. But if they dominate our attempts to understand, we face "the despotism of fact." The subtleties which govern how facts are formed and reformed and how they are developed to hold a mode which we can grasp, these subtleties are of such depth that they allow new meanings every day, else learning mathematics would make theoretical physicists of us all -- or theologians.

Buoyed by the optimism of the Modern world's announced agenda, we took 'Progress' to be automatic, or at least to be inevitable if we followed Hegel, even though its path combined destruction with advance. Today, no historical dialectic seems to lead us logically to 'progress', even though we cannot deny advance, as medicine and physics and biology open access to human self-governance by opposing natural inevitabilities. As Yeats again expressed it: "...progress is a miracle, and it is sudden."(p.178) When theoretical advance comes, of course, it must build on earlier advance. But the bearer of the progress in theory does not seem to appear automatically or inevitably but rather suddenly. Any new insight is amazing in its challenge, which is why it is so often rejected or not fully understood in its day of origin. So the Modern world which so opposed religious 'miracles', the unique and individual supposed violation of a fixed law of nature, now finds its own theoretical advance not obvious but coming as an exemption to the ruling 'laws'. Novel theory rests on the reversal of the expected, with the same upsetting qualities of 'miracle'.

Rather than finding science's progress and our human progress by moving further away from primitive states toward ever increasing 'civilization', we find that the innovations of the day live in their mental lives "...nearer to chaos, every man's desire..."(p.178) "They had imaginative passions because they did not live within our own straight limits."(*Ibid.*) The minds of such innovators live "far out" and must be driven by "imaginative passions". Their minds move "...from this passionate, turbulent reaction against the despotism of fact..."(p.182) We cannot leave mythology behind, as we hoped to because of its imprecision, "...for every new fountain of legend is a new intoxication for the imagination of the world."(p.187) The scientific mind may not seem in its theory to produce what the artistic mind does in its created objects. But we miss the excitement, the miracle, the chaos of the world, if we do not see that the imaginative source of insight springs from the same source for both.

The Modern world, even though at first seeming to domesticate God and the life of divinity to its own level, as in Descartes' "clear and distinct idea" of God, soon becomes suspicious of religion as undermining its own intended completion and seizure of fire from the gods. Religion spoke in legends, which only the insensitive try to interpret as fact, thus demeaning their status and their power. To feel that it could be otherwise stems from our Modern hubris. Yet now as we seek the source of the insights of science and find that they cannot come from facts and indeed may be blocked by the despotism of fact, we suddenly see that the religious era has not been left behind, the Age of Faith inevitably replaced by the Age of Reason. Rather, as reason progressed beyond the obvious, its powerful theorists must, "...as religious thought has always done, utter themselves through legends."(*Ibid.*) We had diverted the flow of legend formation that had spawned religion and poetry and story. It's material now concerned the formation of physical universe and the inner life of atoms, but it origin and inspiration involved a parallel "intoxication of the imagination."

The outward world seemed to yield to scientific assessment, particularly when knowledge was placed in mathematical form. Realizing the threat which the often violent inner life of man posed to the assumption of our command over nature, we attempted to complete its clarification (Descartes) or its improvement (Spinoza) or to tie it inexorable to fact (Locke). But the poet "does not live by bread alone," i.e., by external observation. And Yeats reports that he "...lost the desire of describing outward things." (p.189) Mathematicians, physicists, biochemists are not simply 'describing outward things'. Although it is not quite the inner life they describe either. The similarity between the poet's inward explorations and the scientific theorist's constructions are not far apart and may often be parallel. The chaos of our inner life disturbs and challenges them both to subdue it into verbal and theoretical form. Thus, our understanding can approach that divine level to which only the priest formerly was allowed access.

Philosophy certainly had its role in the formation of the agenda for the Modern Era, as much in political democracies as in the explosion of scientific theory. But then, as so often happens, the theory that opens doors also closes them, if it is allowed to achieve the status of dogma, just as religion genius is stunted when what it terms 'revelations' are taken as dogma. So philosophers become fixed and exist as a block to our advance when they do not challenge themselves and their assumptions constantly, an ancient task still needed. If philosophy thus serves its function to liberate us from reigning theories as well as from facts as despots, it becomes creative, or at least it serves as one spur to creativity, and so allows us "...to escape form weariness by philosophy"(p.193). But of course, to serve this function, one as useful to theoretical advance in the sciences as in the arts, philosophers must see their relationship to poetry, in their formation of insightful words and in a willingness to deal with the chaos in our inner life and not connect it with an imagined fixity.

C. AN AGE OF IMAGINATION

It is hard to imagine what our age of scientific discovery and theory formation might have been like without the use of imagination, in spite of all the early modern stress on fact and clarity. Yeats tells us that in his time "...the age of criticism is about to pass, and an age of imagination, of emotion, of words, of revelation, is about to come in its place"(p.197). Unfortunately, he also adds that "...the solemn voice of men and things...cannot be heard amidst the idle uproar of acts of violence"(p.198). The Age of Reason hoped to eliminate violence by eliminating emotion and moods and also revelations. So that if our time has been scientifically, artistically creative (the two often go together), we have some notion of why we have also witnessed such violence, in spite of all the promises of utopias and the dawn of peace.

As a poet, Yeats has a positive outlook on the Age of Emotion, in contrast to the Age of Reason which hoped to eliminate emotion, or at least to transform it. "We will learn again," he says "that the great passions are angels of God."(p.191) Right enough, much as an age of science thought it would not hear from God again. But angels can become satans and, very unfortunately, destruction seems to have been original in God's design, at least as Darwin has described it. "There is no excellent beauty without strangeness," Yeats notes (p.207), so a purging Puritan purity may restrict our openness to revelations of beauty. Our world in its creativeness cannot escape the wildness and destruction of its originating process, it would seem, if Darwin is at all correct. In our time, the species have become relatively stable to our perception. But Darwin's imaginative revelation of our more than rude origins gives us reason to suspect that the "mask of reason" still hides "acts of violence" not far beneath its calm face. The power of our emotion's imagination can release this as a side effect.

The Modern world wrote its human dreams as a 'comedy', a Frank Capra movie on a world-wide human scale beyond Hollywood's ability to imagine. But tragedy, which the Greeks saw as the other face of comedy, was not to be so easily left behind, given new visions of our human origin. If struggle had produced us, if violence and waste are a necessary part of our creation, civilizations could still be produced as our imaginative achievements. Yet they would always rest on their uncivilized origins, and these could all too easily re-emerge, given the needed driving force of emotion in all discovery and creation, whether scientific or artistic. "Tragedy must always be a drowning and breaking of the dikes that separate man from man..."(p.241) So as technology brought races and cultures into immediate proximity, Yeats would expect tragedy to return (as it has). Thus comedy could not be reason's sole result.

How could Yeats have known in advance of the Achilles heel of Communist aspirations for utopian societies when he said "All movements are held together more by what they hate than by what they love."(p.249) And with the passing of Communism's threat of violence , he explains the disintegration of American unity, once there is no common enemy to hate. 'Love' has been promoted by (some) Christians as a powerful human force, even a divine characteristic. But unfortunately, as our history shows, hate and envy and ambition appear to be even more basic forces, often working for good but just as likely for evil and destruction. Love does not seem able to hold groups together for creative purpose as strongly as hate holds people together for eventual violence. The motives of Marx and Lenin were lofty: the release from suffering of the subjugated masses. But the power of the movement, which became world-wide, stemmed more from its hatred of other groups than from its compassion for the powerless. Thus, hatred breeds a violence that turns to tragedy.

In the insightful Greek legend, Prometheus stole fire from the gods. The Modern Age of Science and Reason appropriated all fire originally thought to belong to the gods, or to the privileged, but they were sure that their newly sophisticated methods would tame power to work "For constructive purposes only." Such has not been the case. We have been creative; we have been innovative, but we have not been able to tame fire power for solely beneficial purposes. Even the Nobel prize draws its resources from gun powder. "...of a certainty Promethian fire will burn some one's fingers," Yeats warns.(p.278) And unfortunately receiving burned fingers was only the beginning of the negative fall-out of the power that passed into Modern hands. Yet our only alternative is to cease to be creative, for all of us to become "flower children," since "...all things are made by the struggle of the individual and the world,"(p.288), as Yeats comments and as Darwin had described before him.

D. THE ART OF THE UNSEEN

A religious age somehow felt that only God remained unseen. In point of fact our inner life, as well as the world of science and of art, deals largely with what remains unseen, even when it is effectively symbolized. Freud was not successful in reducing our collective unconscious entirely to verbal visibility. Symbols, even Freudian symbols, remain crucial for our access to what neither eye hath seen nor ear hath heard nor hand hath touched. Art for instance, Yeats reminds us, "has never taken more than its symbols from anything that the eye can see nor the hand can measure" (p.304). For Empiricism, this is a particularly crucial matter, since Yeats says that what is visually or tactically before us does not yield a literal truth of anything important to us. Yet it can serve as a symbol for what is not so physical, if we do not try to force it to literal use. Why must this be so? Because "...we are seeking to express what no eye has ever seen."(*Ibid.*)

For the Rationalist as well as Empiricist this is equally important, since their philosophies are separated by far less distance than the English Channel. However, they have been seen as fierce rivals, each vying to codify truth from us. Both wanted surface phenomenon as a basis, particularly since Rationalists either avoided the unconscious or sought to translate it fully into something directly accessible to us. In contrast, scientific theory has moved rapidly away from anything directly visible into a realm accessible only to a rare imaginative gift. Thus, a theoretical physicist exploring cosmology knows that what can be discerned by the eye, or what can be rendered consistent with everyday reason, can serve for nothing more than symbols for the uncertain reality it sought to express in uncertain truth. 'Truths' were produced, wide ranging and often powerful, but none is stable beyond replacement or the erosion of time in ways that exclude the intrusion of chaotic elements.

Artistic form could capture, or at least represent, such symbolic intrusion into a subterranean unseen world. On the other hand, print, particularly journalism, could easily turn into a most ignoble power, "...the art of repeating a name again and again with such ridiculous evil association"(p.312). And such popular or verbal distortions were not missing from our philosophies, since we had insisted that words could be made to be true in explaining significant questions. This seemed to remove the questions themselves, because words can be accepted as literally defined. 'Experience' became the key term replacing 'being' as that which we sought to express, since it was supposed that experience could be made to bear the truth, at least as Phenomenology sought to present it even if not in a strict Empiricist sense. This could only be done by reducing 'experience' to a questionable surface simplicity. Since at its frequently seriously disturbing level, 'experience' symbolized darkness more than light.

This is perhaps best illustrated when Yeats says that "...literature is a child of experience always, of knowledge never."(p.317) Literature in all ages and for all peoples, whether written or orally presented, has captured what seems of greatest significance to us. But as Gillian Beer pointed out for us earlier, Darwin's theories, perhaps most revolutionary in their human implications, are developed more along the lines of a novel's plot than as a factual amassing of pure data. Thus, 'knowledge', in its literal sense of what is clearly known to us (which many associate with truth's primary quality), is not the source of our invaluable world literature. This stems from experience, true, but from our imaginative and artistic exploration of the depths of our experience and, even more, our very being, never its surface.

If a philosophy that seeks to convey truth in its theories is to be formed, what must be its source, from what level must it originate? If what is unseen, which now compromises so much of the scientific and the humanistic world, is to be given expression, its forms must be more akin to art than to what is immediate to our visual field -- or even to Kant's Forms of the Understanding. Kant knew this to be true, and in the Third Critique he tentatively explored art's revelatory powers. But he was still intimidated by the Modern expectation to complete knowledge in universal form. Being unable to accept truth as uncertain, he could not see art, or our aesthetic experience, as central to philosophical exploration rather than peripheral. Yeats, on the other hand, has 'philosophy' "...created out of anxiety for sympathy..."(p.323), which reflects Existentialism's approach as well.

To an age searching to find truth in history, at least since Hegel's time, Yeats knows that"...all art is the disengagement of a soul from place and history."(p.339) We, on the other hand, have for at least two centuries been trying to understand everything by setting it in its historic setting. We have either absolutized this with Hegel or radically relativized truth when we find it impossible to interpret history in universally acceptable categories. If art is crucial to philosophical understanding, and if all art does in fact disengage the soul from place and history, then 'history' is perhaps a false setting for our search for truth, exciting as its voyeurism may be to the provincial who has not let his or her mind circle "around the world in eighty days". In *Letters to A Young Poet*, Rilke explains to the would-be author of literature or poetry that it is not necessary to expand individual experience by the historical quest in order to state or to discover something true. That lies within the imaginative individual in his or her inner artistic exploration.

Yeats perhaps gives us a hint of how uncertain truth is formed when he defines insight as "...a well ordered incident in the mythology of his imagination."(p.358) Imagination shapes mythology, obviously, but the key is the "well ordered incident." Much of our life, whether imaginative or factual, is disordered, tending to chaotic patterns. But some aspects become well ordered and thus both potentially insightful as well as insight bearing and symbolic of truth. Philosophical women and men often distrust instinct, because it disturbs contemplation, which was Aristotle's goal for thought. Practical men, pragmatists, merchants, gamblers, distrust everything they cannot use "in the routine of immediate events."(p.339). In contrast, impulse and the method of creation can only be learned from "the criticism of poets."(*Ibid.*). This is done by exploring the interior paths and their constructed forms open to us, not simply accepting a supposed surface or ordinary meaning. There is an excitement in some movements of the artistic life which must be captured. This leads us to the art of the unseen, to an uncertain truth.

E. THE REFERENCE OF OUR DREAMS

Could Freud have established his crucial assumptions, that our dreams refer only to traumatic but to factual events in our forgotten childhood, dreams could be pinned down to factual reference. But in fact our dreams are constructed more of fictional truth. Thus, we must seek the reference of our dreams elsewhere than in our literal experience. Of course, should they prove to be wholly fictional, we could reduce them to nursery rhyme status. But we cannot escape the fact that what they open to us is a world which is equally 'real', in a metaphysical sense (i.e. that which underlies experience and is assumed by us rather than what is initially examined) and so perhaps could contain more truth than we have fully explored. Surely to read the current cosmologies offered by theoretical physics is to enter a literal dream world -- yet one perhaps more real than our life in the daylight.

We have explored our natural languages via linguistics and wanted ordinary language to establish certain truth for us. Unfortunately for these neat solutions Yeats reports: "Allegory and, to a much greater degree, symbolism are a natural language."(p.368) Yet if so, truth begins to recede from simplicity, finality, and directness. If the Modern World wanted to reject myth, it also lost the soul's magnificence, since allegory and symbolism are the 'natural language' by which the soul "when entranced or even in ordinary sleep, communes with God and the angels."(*Ibid.*) If we do not admit this, it is we who limit and trivialize our powers of communication, cutting off all converse with divinities. For in the approach which Yeats recommends, "one can speak of things which cannot be spoken of in any other language" (*Ibid.*). We may sometimes approach the Ark. We may feel a sense of 'unreality' when such language is used to describe things which can be announced as well in ordinary words. Yet this sense of unreality should not be a cause for rejection but for further investigation.

History has been studied for over a century as the key to understanding, but Nietzsche objected to 'historical understanding' as too limiting to our creativity. We need to retain, to revive, an antique frenzy. In contrast, history becomes a conscious art (vs. instinctive) which makes us articulate but then destroys our old 'wild energy'(p.373). To rationalize history is to see ourselves as further along in progress in time, as Hegel thought he was. Yet at the same moment it cuts us off from Dionysian frenzy, that which is still the key to insight and thus to truth. The Moderns have made themselves pedestrians in a rapidly expanding space age. "They seek not forbidden treasures, they know not how to cast nets." (p.395) Our problem is not to distance ourselves from our cultural ancestors but to retain, to revitalize, their more instinctive vital energies.

F. ROMANTICISM RESTORED

'Romanticism', in its unpopular image, usually refers to a vague sentimentalism, one drifting far from reality in a make-believe world. But Plato long ago recognized that all the important terms in our vocabulary have multiple meanings and that it is well worth our while to search out a more substantive use for a popular and disputed term. Yeats gives us a lead in this process. "The romantic tradition," he says "with its turbulent heroism, its self-assertion, is over, superseded by a new naturalism that leaves man helpless before the contents of his own mind."(p.405) Of course, for some time to argue for 'naturalism' to replace a turbulent heroism would have been taken for granted to be the arrival of common sense. One could settle down raw emotion and get at nature unclouded. But as 'self-assertion' was left-behind, did the creative individual also fade as our key to insight?

Again, the status of myth is important , and we knew that the Romantic spirit is inspired by myth. Yeats cites Vico: "We should reject all philosophy that does not begin in myth..."(p.409) This is the opposite of the claim that we must 'demythologize' everything, that is, render it neat and incapable of inspiring. Simple men and women provide a universal base -- Yeats agrees that much with "ordinary language" philosophy (p.448). But their 'unchanging experience' undergirds civilizations that make vastly different assumptions in their beliefs. This is a universalism of common myth and foundational story, not one of common reason or sense experience. And we know that the zest of romanticism lies behind such an assurance about common experience. Neither reason nor sense experience can provide such a basis, universal as each appears to be, since the commonalty of experience lies in its use of inspirational myth, not in fact.

Romantics, too, do not live a life of calm (one might say dull) reason and sense experience. Depths do not lie on that level, and it is the depth behind surface experience that we need to reach. "I think," says Yeats, "profound philosophy [vs. common sense] must come from terror. An abyss opens under our feet."(p.502) Romantics experience terror as well as calm and so at least have an opportunity to reach profundity. Existentialism will come along to stress the experience of 'nothingness' as that which opens insight, so that standing on too solid ground can prove to be a liability. Rationality moves heaven and earth to erase or to reconcile contradictions. The Romantic prizes them because he or she feels they bring him closer to understanding, although there is nothing certain about this. This is because "reality is expressed in a series of contradictions."(p.503), not as yielding to the reconciliation of a Hegelian dialectic but as revealing our permanent human condition, that is, "beyond progress."

Both Rationalism and Empiricism, we know, sought to escape emotion or else to transform it into a form of rational understanding. Poetic speech cannot do that, else it loses its vitality. A poem is an elaboration of the rhythms of common speech and their association with profound feelings. Analytical philosophy stressed 'common speech,' but it did not explore any poetic elaboration which would have disturbed its surface clarity. In addition to its surface meanings, Yeats is convinced that common speech reveals 'rhythms' which associate with feelings. Thus, followed far enough, we do not escape emotion by studying common speech. Rather, we should be lead to profound, not simple, feelings. Emotion, then, is the originating power of an significant speech and can only be eliminated at the risk of rendering our speech innocuous.

'Hatred' does not appear much in Modern Philosophy, since it is disturbing of calm finality. But distortions which blocks our insight, Yeats feels, are properly responded to by hatred. "I hate and still hate," he says "with an ever growing hatred the literature of the point of view." (p.511) The Romantic temperament wants truth to be revealed by passion. And oddly, they feel that they can reach a level of universalism with the emotions and with mythic creation, non-literate and indirect as this may be. Thus, literature of the "point of view" is, oddly, a provincialism, because it asserts the possibility of a single understanding. Yeats might respond similarly to the suggestion that "all things are gendered " or that we should express only that which conforms to the "politically correct" thought of the day. Universalism can never be found on the surface of experience; that is too time-bound. But the unseen inner depths of life and of our physical universe can break the bond of any "point of view."

Poetry as a vehicle should be the key in our approach here, he argues. And this is not so far from our "ordinary speech" as the advocate of finality in philosophy might think. He says: "I tried to make the language of poetry coincide with that of passionate, normal speech."(p.521) But the first thing we need to note is that 'normal speech' is often not calm but is passionate, as the daily newspapers reports of struggles testify. Thus, in its passionate mode as 'average' speech, our language is not far from poetry but rather close. The Irish are famous for finding romantic exaggeration more insightful than literal report. Yeats for certain is an Irish poet, but is his insight into the origin of passionate poetry a better key to understanding, as well as to our expression of all that lies hidden from general view? It is unseen, but in many ways it is more in control of our lives, and thus of 'truth', than any report of surface experience or the operation of reason could be.

Chapter YII. THE DESIGNER OF THE LOCKS HOLDS THE UNAVAILABLE KEYS

To suggest that the above is true is not to return to the "watch maker" argument which claims to "prove" God's existence. That thesis wanted you to look at the intricacies of design in the world and to exclaim: "Then, there exists a designer! " As Thomas Aquinas pointed out, you are not required to make such a response if you accept Nature as it is, if you do not demand non-natural causes to explain what is seen. Only those who begin by wanting explanations, other than a description of what lies before them and how it functions, are likely to make that mental move . Moreover, any such inference which is drawn from the world we see does not lead directly to a "Christian God", a Being with personal characteristics capable of love and concern. The world we know exhibits only a little of those qualities. In fact, it more often appears cold, impersonal, and prone to destruction.

A majority of human beings feel inhibited, one might even say "locked" within their limitations which they find difficult to remove or to overcome. Some of these blocks are obviously physiological, inborn, the result of individual genetic inheritance, flaws or major malfunctions in the physiological system. Beyond these obvious defects, some of which can be

partially overcome, however, there are the psychological, emotional, even mental limitations and unknowns that seem to thwart the full expression of those powers which, great or small, have been given to us. We struggle to find avenues of expression, verbal, physical, artistic. And occasionally, we "find the right key". Then the imaginative, insightful products of our release can be impressive. But this is true for only a very few people in any public way. Unsung heroes, male and female, may be more plentiful privately, of course.

Our major question, the one which thwarts us in our relation to "the designer of these locks," is to decide whether there are many different locks or really only one; and if we accept that the locks are multiple, whether one master key fits all; or whether there are an indefinite variety of keys, some fitting one lock only, others which fit several and, to our frustration, some keys which in fact unlock nothing of significance that we can locate. These would be the keys for locks never imposed upon us or upon any actually created universe, presumably. As we grapple with this important issue, our basic question of approach is whether the lock designer is a Rationalist, since the very existence of multiple locks and our "key problem" assures us that Empiricism was not the operative theory in design. Something remains hidden from us which no immediate experience can disclose, and it is vital to our human welfare to come to conclusions that no sense experience can reveal.

To return to the question of a possible Rationalist designer: this option seems unlikely, given the presence of locks which have no known key, plus the existence of keys which open no known locks, and the oddity we encounter in the match up of keys to locks. The pattern is not that of a Rationalist. It defies logic; or that is, there is no final logic to the match-up. More important, no manuals of instruction were issued with our natural order, or even with the more tidy logical-mathematical order. It was not 'rational' to place us here within such an odd design, knowing that without a handbook it would take us centuries to discover elementary things about Nature's operation. Any designer who failed to provide explicit instructions, we would say, is not fully rational and may in fact be partly irrational, considering the immensity of what we were expected to discover, and given the suffering we have had to undergo due to our original lack of knowledge about Nature and our slowness in acquiring it.

Sometimes we do receive what various religions call 'revelations'; these are insights into the designer's intent in constructing the-locks-that-bind and what we are expected to do about it, as well as about that divinity's intentions towards us and our future. In the Modern Era, this form of disclosure precipitated a clash between most religions and the programs of the Enlightenment, Rationalist, Scientific and/or Empirical world views. According to any of those outlooks, no God of any religious significance was needed or necessary. And even more important, there was no way to account for why a God would give anyone a "revelation', since these go only to certain persons, not to all. Those dominant philosophies were all universalistic in their outlook, associated as they often were with democratic political theories. Since the development of each of these philosophies and social theories offered much good to the human race. After we had experienced centuries of subjugation and human suffering, they seemed to offer solutions to human ills preferable to those offered by most religions, just because they allowed us individual self-determination and universal knowledge.

How, then, could any religious view ever gain popularity again among an "enlightened" people? That prospect seemed to involve a contradiction. This dilemma is connected to the question of the locks we still need to unlock, how we find the key or keys, and the intent of the Designer of the-locks-that-bind. According to all the philosophers associated with the Enlightenment and with Modern Science and Democracy, with diligence we should eventually be able to find a single master key. Then we could watch ourselves increasingly come together as various peoples uniting to effect our release from all that inhibits us. This has happened to some modest extent and has provided immense benefits to some fortunate groups. But the full "secret of the lock design" proved not to be that easy to solve.

The main problems which the pioneers of our self liberation (in itself an admirable notion) ran into were two:

1)	The men and women who were to be released failed to come into sustained theoretical and/or practical unity, not for even what seemed to be so attractive a goal; in increasing numbers we were still held captive by old hatreds, greeds and power-seeking that sought domination and refused cooperation (which is the main requirement for these philosophies to succeed in their goals); and

2)	in spite of an impressive scientific, philosophical search based on the "one master key" approach, no single theory seemed able to establish itself finally and exclusively. Furthermore, the world to be explained, both scientific and human, grew in complexity and diversity rather than toward simplicity, in spite of immense scientific, theoretical advance. Finding ourselves blocked, since the future of these scientific, philosophical, and political theories had not worked out as projected, we began to suspect that the Designer of the locks had not used so simple a unified plan as had been supposed.

We know that many of the locks confronting us can be opened, since we have done this progressively, in medicine, mathematics, physics, biology, etc. But what perhaps first raised our suspicion that the master key might not be as accessible to us as we had thought was that the unlocking of the locks that bind the human mind and personality did not seem to parallel other physical advances, a desirable result which we had projected. True, we could distinguish between primitive superstitions and Modern intelligence. But the drives that erupted in the souls of men and women, and the return of the suspicion that we might have 'souls' capable of good and evil as well as bodies and minds, seemed to frustrate all plans for our total, final release.

This failure of our early optimism is not due solely to some human stubbornness, or even to our self-destructive, self-frustrating tendencies, although these did not disappear even in highly sophisticated societies. Theories, which we counted on to provide the keys for our release, seemed either not to be fully explanatory or to be one-sided and not complete. 'Empiricism' clarified much, but unfortunately much also grew in importance that seemed not immediately accessible to the five senses. Scientists and mathematicians, ironically, became the least empirical in theory of all. 'Rationalism' is preferable rather than to think that the world is not fully open to penetration by the human mind, but the inner life did not yield the clarity and finality which Rationalism seemed to demand. 'Democracy' spread, to the benefit of millions. But it also was not preferred by millions who saw it only as a loss of their power over others, or as a requirement that they not take what they could by their strength and ingenuity -- although fashion sometimes dictated that aspiring tyrants give lip service to democracy's virtues.

Science, oddly, became the leader in abandoning the single master key theory. For at least a century scientific advance had provided the clearest demonstration, or so it seemed, that the eventual union of all theories into one comprehensive master theory would be achieved. In other words, it proceeded on the conviction that there is one key (quite complex of course) for all the locks that need to be opened, for both our theoretical and for our personal release. Yet theory succeeded theory, each more intriguing than the one before, and depth succeeded depth, while the extent of our universe itself seemed to 'explode'. We found that some fascinating keys seemed to open no locks but were more like self-contained puzzles, such as certain areas in mathematics and logic. We found that some locks could be opened by several keys, not simply by one. Theory became more powerful, fascinating in its depth, but not necessarily finally unified or unifiable.

One increasing suspicion grew: the Designer of the locks had not only held all the keys at the start of our exploration to discover avenues for our release and self-control, but he/she
clearly had operated on a system of keys that is more complex than our Modern theories had supposed and not so neat in its plan as we had hoped. We had forgotten to ask if the Designer of both the locks and their keys really did operate as a divinity according to the rules of Rationalism, Empiricism, the Enlightenment, or even Democracy. Since all of these outlooks had improved our lot in the Modern Era, we could not suppose that the Designer of the keys could be opposed to our adopting them as operative theories, since these approaches opened up so much of benefit, particularly in medicine and in the sciences. Yet these attractive philosophies could not possibly form the whole basis of the Designer's intent, since the locks were not opening as neatly or as progressively as many had projected.

Were there even locks for which no key had been made available, no matter if they remained hidden from sight for centuries, such as for instance one that would control the human soul with its greed, jealousy and often hidden quest for power? Freud saw 'dreams' as revelatory in this way. We had sometimes been able to deal with these interior obstacles by converting a few souls to one religion or another based on peace or love. However, the results of this change were still individual not universal, while our public problems were of universal proportions.

Would new keys always be found, even in science, to replace old keys, or theories, that is, keys which had once worked (e.g., Newtonian physics, Marx) but now seem not to be exclusive? If the key system itself was subject to a certain element of chaos, perhaps its comprehension was not as easily obtainable as our early enthusiasm over our releasing discoveries had supposed. We needed an assured necessity in Nature in order to complete our "insight into everything", but the Designer of the locks had perhaps shown more freedom of the will, and even a touch of intrigue and arbitrariness, we began to suspect. This is not so extreme, even if true, as the idea Einstein rejected, that "God's plays dice with the universe." Simplicity, reliability seemed to hold in wide areas, but unfortunately perhaps not in those most important to human peace and order.

The chief incongruity which plagues us, and which we began to suspect was intentional, is that the exploration and content of the human psyche does not parallel our exploration or control of physical space. These two realms do not seem to be constructed on similar plans at all, which frustrates the calm goals of the Enlightenment. Their operations are not 'parallel', as Spinoza had projected. We can extend mathematics only so far. It cannot be used as a universal blueprint eventually to guide all understanding. There seems to be no simple translation of all human languages into one another without residue, which should be possible if they were constructed along a Rationalist's design. Our ultimate hope for universal understanding stops, because there is no single key for it, although there are many which we can and do use. Today we seem to hear: "You don't like that theory? It isn't perfect? Here, try this one." Theories seem not limited in their number, although not infinite, which is both exciting and frustrating, given our quest for completion.

There are flashes of brilliance in our use of words and concepts and languages as symbolic instruments, as evidenced in our poetry and literature. Yet, these structures do not admit of a brilliance of communication and understanding that can be extended to all; only a few prove to be their masters. The majority of us use languages clumsily. The extraordinary understanding they can produce is to be admired, but unfortunately our languages are also the cause of endless miscommunication. Only a very few can become skilled in their analysis and in their clarifying use. Our theories about them, and about all things, seem to go on developing without end, rather than reaching closure as Aristotle (and Wittgenstein) wanted, since only that would allow the completion of our understanding. Aristotle postulated an Unmoved Mover, whose function it was to hold the mental world together. This was a symbol of the intellectual rest we seek and his preference for contemplation. However, incompleteness and movement seem more to be the Designer's mode of operation, which we too must follow-- else we lock ourselves up in our own mental dreams.

The intellectual ame of Final Comprehension, which we sometimes play and which a few take as an obsession, seems neither to have a single set of rules nor to be so designed that final victory (completion) is possible. Individual chess matches can be won, but not the one which discovers the final scheme for unlocking both the world's and all human secrets, the plans of our design, of our operation, and for all repairs. Like the puzzle put out with an intentional missing piece or two, the system of locks seems to have an intentional scheme of incompleteness. Partial completion of theory and control, yes; 'final solutions', no. And when we try to impose these by force, disaster usually results.

The music begins, the dance goes on; but one's partner never seems to be exactly the same. Of course, we could consider one long-given response to this situation: the belief that *the* key *is* there but is yet to be found. However, as recent theories have developed, the available evidence does not argue for this, considering that two or three centuries of concentrated effort have not led us to it.

Theories do not appear to expand and to develop as a coherence of the whole, which Rationalists and Idealists define as the way of truth. Rather, they move by innovation and by departures which, while not totally inconsistent, may still be at odds with existing theories. Yet as a novel departure, each new theory offers us potential insight and even power for our control, but not as developed along a single consistent line. 'Revelation' in religion comes a little closer to our situation by parallel, since radically innovative and suggestive theories seem to come not simply as "logical extensions" of existing theories, but instead as radical departures suggested by some unclear aspect in a functioning theory. And all major theories of any magnitude seem capable of being used as a basis upon which the world can be grasped and explored, not just one. In this case, we can expect future theories still unformulated to suggest provocative insights into the world's structure, but this does not mean that the movement is towards a single all-encompassing theory, not at all.

What of our future and the powerful Modern hope to reshape the human situation? What about the future of our religions? We know that the historic attempts to remake a whole people, e.g., in the USSR, China, Viet Nam etc., although able to produce certain changes have largely been judged to be failures, because terror, repression and a vast destruction of lives often went with this and undermined any positive outcome (c.f., the "Cultural Revolution" in China). We know that projected benefits to human society cannot result from arousing hatred for any group, class, race, or sex. Whenever tried on a small scale, much of the Christian doctrine of loving and forgiving one's enemies seems empirically proven to be practical. But if we eventually face our same human nature, with its traditional virtues, powers, and faults, then education, enlightenment, scientific power placed in our hands, can result in great benefit, whether in medicine, technology, or the arts. But tragically these advances also often increase our powers of physical destruction and self-destruction, rather than eliminating them.

If we cannot any longer base our future on the premise of a mass transformation of human nature, democracies, educational programs can still lift a people up, expand opportunities and develop human potential, now at last for both sexes. But such advances are never free from challenge and loss, always subject to complications and the reasserting of totalitarian control and the attempted censorship of free expression, even in the name of 'good' causes and the righting of wrongs. Individuals can be dramatically altered, improved, released, but by religions and philosophies as much as by new social/scientific theories. We cannot promote any one path as the single route to human betterment, since such cannot be found free of challenge. No one can offer a totally "clean" record. Diversity in approach has a weakness which centralized control does not have, but diversity's ineffectiveness makes it less liable to be abused by autocrats and demagogues.

If religions return as a still human option, one that the Modern Era can no longer rule out by its unified Utopian vision of the power of the sciences or by a belief in irreversible 'progress', the superstitions, the hatreds, and the repression that religious groups have bred in the past need not return. We can chart the benefit of Judaic, Christian, Muslim belief as well as Hinduism, Confucianism, and Buddhism,

Zen or otherwise. But their 'crimes', inflicted in the name of preserving a purity in religious doctrine, can be documented too; and the gift of the Enlightenment is to enable us to reject that part of religion which we find destructive. Yet, religious belief itself cannot be put on the Enlightenment basis, since that works better for educational and political institutions than for religious traditions which involve revelations not universal in their distribution. Like the multiplicity of keys for a not identical set of locks, we ought not to expect to unite religions into one doctrine if one cannot unify all the sciences.

We realize, of course, that we face a Designer of the locks who must possess the central characteristics of personality. To explore 'possible worlds' makes perfect sense to recent cosmologists. Thus, someone had to make a choice, had to possess a decisive and an enforceable power; otherwise we would not face this particular universe -- either none or uncontrolled chaos. More important, since the locks that hold back access and the information we need could have been unified and a simplified instruction "Manual for Nature" included, some 'will' was necessarily active, else we would not face the particular combination of rational structure together with its inconsistencies which we do. Nothing about the design, neither the locks nor the keys nor our understanding, requires that the Designer of the locks be loving or concerned or forgiving. The universe does not often show us that face, although it does not show a total hostility towards our needs either. Religions, then, can offer revelations about other aspects of the Designer, ones not universally distributed or easily read off of Nature's plan. "Natural Religion" involves a non-sequitur.

The convenient premise of universality holds only in limited areas and, even when achieved, seems inherently unstable, since no single key unlocks all or excludes all other proposed insights and theories, that is, 'keys'. We know 'Rationalism' to be attractive, if it were true, but it seems to hold only in limited areas and rather totally to miss the most important creative, and difficult, aspects of human personality. These involve our inner life, our tendencies to destruction and malevolence, as well as to rational discussion and construction. 'Empiricism' is a clarifying approach, but again it seems to work better in simple matters, not complex. Chaos, unconscious forces, block its application. It also misses totally the speculative construction of mathematics, physics, cosmology, and increasingly even biology, as it moves away from classification towards the exploration of intricate structures. The 'Enlightenment' can aid education; it can reduce the restrictions previously placed on the mind's arenas of investigation.

Yet it seems to miss the sources of human creativity and profundity, as well as failing to see that religions are not universal in their source, and so not capable of being reduced to a common plane. The Designer seems to have given final preference to individuality, much as Kierkegaard suspected.

Fundamental to our recently changed situation is the fact that all the sources for the conditions we face, that is, of our own creativity and violence and religious insight, do not lie on the common plane of reason. 'Transcendence' returns as a crucial concept, since so much has escaped us which we intended to domesticate to our grasp and to our control. The powers of some of our developed comprehensions are great and our abilities in many areas have increased, e.g. in psychiatry. Still the lack of a final unity of plan on the plane of universal understanding, the important inbreaking of esoteric insights closed but to the few, our failure to domesticate the depths of the human spirit for good and for ill -- each testifies to much that lies beyond any immediate access.

A great deal, but not all, of the power once transferred from God to man can now be returned to the Designer of the locks. Those of us with keys that unlock certain forms of knowledge and its resulting power cannot be asked to return them. They have passed to us more or less permanently. The Naturalist may still find power to lie only within Nature, but at least it is possible once again to see a great deal of control retained by the one who knows which locks can be opened, which ones are extremely difficult and which, indeed, seemed blocked off. Nicholas of Cusa spoke of a "learned ignorance" in relation to our inquiries into God's nature. That notion now returns with a greater power and significance than Cusanus could have imagined. He meant that, as we learn about God, we simultaneously become all the more aware of how much still remains dark in the divine nature. Our learning about God can be real, but it also increases our awareness of how much we do not know. Our ignorance had been our bliss.

What does "learned ignorance" mean today in our relationship to the Designer of the Locks, if we renounce the hubris of the Modern quest for the universal openness of all knowledge? One thing which the realization that we do not possess all the keys to all the locks brings to us is the conviction that we do not now, and possibly never will, have all the answers to all the problems we need in order to create a Utopia, perhaps not even for individual selves let alone for vast peoples. The realization of this residual, continual 'ignorance' is indeed 'learned', since by it we comprehend something of the "true human situation" and must/should give up the Modern illusion that we can totally recreate ourselves. The original Descent of Man has given us, in time, many powers, just as Darwin projected, but we do not by any means have all we need. We have added to our capabilities spectacularly. Unfortunately, we still retain a strong tendency to defeat/ destroy ourselves.

Sadly, as the aftermath of the disillusionment over -- not the total loss but the limiting of our powers which we once projected to be unlimited -- we face a time of repression, of the censorship of all who do not share a particular view. This is in many ways worse than the reign of political/military tyrants and despots, because it comes from the revolutionary left, in silent rage and reaction against the loss of their dream of vast human transformations. It is a sad story of our recent Fall, worse than Adam and Eve in the Garden of Eden, since that represented defiance against God. But God having been removed or rendered incompetent, human rage now takes intellectual, often hidden forms, because it is really against ourselves and the loss of our Modern dreams. It is Prometheus now turned upon himself, having stolen a great deal but not all of the divine fire and not having found it as totally liberating as he had hoped. Can we, in the recently encountered restrictions that govern our powers for change, learn again to live with those who are not like ourselves in thought and disposition? We must, since we know that all of our fellows will not be made uniform or to our liking, neither in theory nor in behavior, except by self-defeating violence.

If we lack the key to every secret we expected to unlock, this defines the major social/political/philosophical test we face. And mystery returns to a center position. Now obscurity is not all in God's nature. We do not know why the Designer of the locks has held back certain keys, some perhaps forever, or why we have been allowed access to vast powers, only to find that even these acquisitions were subject to time-delay and great human loss. More importantly, we do not know why the design of the locks is not laid out on a coordinated, unified, totally consistent plan. Why are our theories often so at odds; why do they not fit all that is in the world like the product of a factual design? Because, we begin to suspect as Yeats reports and as our insights into nature's fantastic depths beyond directly observable fact increasingly confirms, because the form of Nature itself evolved. What we now explore had no original pre-established design (thus no pre-established harmony, Leibniz).

As our imagination is challenged at every turn by scientific discovery which makes what formerly were thought to be 'facts' seem constantly new, our optimism that the laws of nature would open all the locks plaguing human nature is gone and we can afford to be generous in accepting non-conformity. We thought we could provide enough for all, or that we would soon learn how to do so. Yet as restrictions on our lives return, or that is as this becomes evident, it is coupled with the haunting suspicion that this time we do not have the prospect of breaking all the codes. We may have to learn to coexist with handicaps. No matter if we have learned how to remove some (although mostly the physical) of our limitations, we too often draw back from final cooperation to be sure that "I" at least get "mine". Old suspicions arise about the "threat" posed by anyone who does not agree with us, or who seems not like us, or is not bound to our cause. Jesus did say "He who is not for me is against me", but he intended it primarily spiritually. We have tended to take this phrase literally, moving to exclude, if not to destroy, all whom we do not perceive as "with us".

Since the meanness of the human spirit, in spite of its expansive generosities at moments, has not been eliminated (Jesus feeding of the 5000 doesn't scratch the surface), we fear we may again degenerate into constant quarreling rather than working together for such cooperation as we can achieve. 'Compromise' does not appear as desirable as it did at the origin of democratic theory. Sharing power voluntarily becomes more difficult although not impossible. Selfishness looms large, as the socialist/communist dreams prove not possible to implement radically without the use of a tyranny that corrodes the ideal. The unavailable keys held in the hands of the Designer of the Locks takes on an air of mystery -- but not malignancy. Our curiosity as to whether the controlling power is really loving or benign or harsh is increased.

If we are to judge by the system of the locks which control our worlds, both those above and inside, about which we have now amassed considerable knowledge, we would be hard pressed to judge the Designer to be 'loving'. True, those aspects of love which are offered to us often are our most rewarding human experiences. But on the whole the lock still remains on our agenda for the "full disclosure" of Nature, particularly the troubling lock still fastened on the recesses of the human mind and spirit. This leads us to think of the lock system as intriguing, challenging, but also as unnecessarily wasteful of life and often destructive of the human spirit. Our "bright moments" are memorable and form the basis for our most moving literature, music, and art. Yet even that considerable creative production evidences an awareness of the evil of destruction; it reflects our proneness to a madness which Freud cannot control and our inhumanity to our fellow creatures, which is often unleashed in the name of self-improvement. The locks and the keying system tell a mixed story of divine intent.

Thus, if we are told that the Designer has an inner nature of love, is capable of self-sacrifice and intends "just rewards" for good and for evil -- this can only come as a revelation, one startling in its contrast to even the most favorable accounts of history, although it is akin to the Utopian theories which held so many in their sway for so long. Those visions were made of human dreams about exercising a power of transformation on self and society, all based on the Modern Era's optimism that all locks soon would open for us. We plotted progress as a non-reversible line forward, based on achieving access to the keys for the remaining locks-that-bind us and on our assumption that a single, coordinated plan for the design of all locks was about to be sketched in. Such, unfortunately, seems to be neither the nature of the master theory (the key design) nor of our ability to provide total release for ourselves.

On the other hand, this makes it more "realistic" to follow the Buddha in believing that human suffering can be overcome, that release is available for those who follow a prescribed path which has been found to dissolve individual suffering. But note that this does not restructure the world or in any way offer to eliminate the continued source of suffering. Rather, it teaches us how to cope with it by more or less drastic (depending on your version of Buddhism) self-discipline. If there were a Designer behind the "Buddha's way", it would be impersonal but still neutral when it comes to allowing us to achieve success fully as individuals. Buddhism does not revolutionize societies or build Utopias, although it can reconstruct an individual follower or small group. It does not suspect that a malignant intent was built into the system of locks, but it projects no notion of 'care' into the design either.

Christian claims for a divinity who is loving and caring and sacrificing and forgiving are not absurd. They simply are not confirmed by our knowledge of the design of the locking system and by the inaccessibility or the unavailability of the keys we need to save ourselves from destruction. Anyone who follows Jesus, or who is even impressed or attracted to his life and work, should feel amazed every time he or she holds the morning newspapers in one hand and the gospel documents in the other. Crucifixion is a logical consequence for one who is oblivious to the tendency of power systems to destroy, or at least to put down, *any* challenger (not just women or some minority race). To "follow" Jesus is truly to "take up a cross", because that way goes counter to the immense rewards which the natural world gives to the successful and the minor rewards which it passes out to those who stay in line to be 'neutralized'.

What of the future, since like Utopian doctrines Christianity of necessity offers a 'futuristic' plan? Modern Utopias brought a bright future within our grasp based on a time-table projected on our new ability to control nature. Christians had, on the other hand, projected their Utopias beyond time. Just as physicists/cosmologists today speculate on the origins of time and give us suggestive accounts, Christians postulated the collapse, the transformation of time as we know it. The present framework cannot provide uniform release, only some bright moments and many dark ones. Just as we now project backwards on the comparatively brief history of time, so Christians must project forward to time's end. It seems as if the Designer of the locking system of Nature, and particularly of that which governs our human nature, did not enter the program of instructions needed to provide a simultaneous opening of all the locks within the present duration of time.

Yet since there were locks imposed, and since we have discovered some keys, and since we came to possess some of these early but many only later in the drama of human history, all is not fixed in the present. We cannot expect, either individually or collectively, a Houdini-like breaking open of all locks in order to provide a release both surprising and unexpected. The flaw, the Achilles heel in the plan of the Modern Era, was to suppose that all the keys could be collected, particularly those for the locks on the human spirit that precipitated our Fall, as Genesis or Kierkegaard or Camus have given us accounts of this still repeating tragedy. Our sense that we have failed and do fail in the human struggle, which need not involve actual betrayal or destruction or a divinity, although it often does, constantly threatens to place the human spirit back in bondage. And the key for our permanent release from this too-often-failure-inducing-experience is still locked away, defying our search. The design is apparently unresponsive to the pain we continue to inflict, on ourselves and on each other.

We could speculate that the locking system (or "unsystem" like the "unbirthday" party of Alice) is controlled by a timing device, set to go off at intervals, and that finally all remaining closures will be released. This is possible and would not be too odd, since in moments of modesty we often feel as if the locks we probe have spontaneously opened to us of themselves, not entirely in response to our investigation and sophisticated increase in knowledge and our new theoretical keys. We call this the genius of discovery. The end would be the beginning in reverse. Instead of all locks simultaneously going into operation by command on a release of power, the end of time's brief history would be the 'Unbang', an implosion, a falling away rather than a gathering together of all operative systems, those governing the various orders of Nature (there seems to be more than one) and the controls over the human psyche and spirit.

However, nothing in our present understanding of either natural or human orders can predict that dramatic happening, or even plot it as a super-event coming within time. From the speculative theories of cosmologists we construct models which say that, like the various possible origins of our universe, there could be various possible "endings" or a basic reordering of designs. Nothing we know about either our universe or our human origins makes that impossible; it is simply a non-confirmable speculative theory of radical alteration, much like that of our coming into being à la Darwin in its speculative postulate.

The Descent of Man could turn into Ascent, if the structures governing our formation were altered radically and abruptly. This option is one of the side benefits of the fact that we now believe we have not always been as we are, although this was realized neither at Darwin's nor at Copernicus' time, due to the hostility aroused by so upsetting a theory. If we have not always been as we now find ourselves, there is no reason why we must remain exactly as we are. Our natures and the locking systems in control developed; they can undevelop. Nature is not eternal, as the Greeks thought , but rather flexible.

The problem with such an optimism, one based on the possibility for a future radical Ascent, is our inability, given the holocausts in the Modern Era, to believe that these alterations can be effected en masse by our concerted efforts. Even our removal of many locks on Nature so long in place, most spectacularly evidenced in the amazing advance of medicine, unfortunately cannot now lead us to an optimism over 'progress' as a gradual release to us of all keys. The locking system is not that favorable to our wishful designs, although quite obviously it has yielded to the opening out of much knowledge. However, our enthusiasm has been radically tempered in recent days by our increasing awareness that the power released to us is not restricted to only "good" uses. We have not stopped destroying ourselves. When new secrets of power have been released, we have often simply responded by escalated evil, that is, propounding purposeless destruction.

One possibility which we are aware of about the intent of the Designer of the locks is that the power which imposed a system, so intriguing, so powerful, so potentially destructive, could reverse and release the whole system of restrictions -- and that the designer must have retained the ability to do so. Religious beliefs become meaningful in a new and significant way in the post-progress, back-to-the-beginning aura which characterizes our age. Why? Because each in its individual nonuniversalizable ways offers an account of how we may still be locked in, plus what we can and cannot do about this. Theistic religions offer hints or even assertions, usually carefully shrouded in symbol and indirection (as is appropriate to our situation of non-certainty), about whether and how the locks might be released for an altered future. Acceptance of any of these future options rests on belief, never on full knowledge. Such unlimited power is not open to us, neither in science nor in philosophy, although degrees of certainty may vary for different areas, as Aristotle pointed out.

Can we engage the Designer of the locks in dialogue, for our edification even if not in the hope of receiving sets of answers? Jews, Muslims, and Christians have certainly thought so. Fascinating as the recorded words of these religious disclosures are, we do not hear one divine voice but several. Fortunately these are not fully at odds. Einstein and a number of physicists since have speculated about knowing "the mind of God". Recent theoretical physics and its speculative hypotheses give us several accounts of this psychoanalysis of divinity. All the scriptures of all religions might be viewed as yet inconclusive divine dialogues, although some ardent disciples, quite oddly, claim a finality to their interchange, in spite of the fact that any divinity transcending Nature could not possibly be available for our comprehension, nor could our speech ever fully express it as such even if 'revealed' to us. 'Dialogues' traditionally are seen as being instructive to serious 'seekers' but not as dogma producing.

We can stand in sacred places, engage in rituals, read the texts of various scriptures (doing so even as Wittgenstein or as Tolstoy might advise to do to achieve clarity), experience our own moments of transcendence, enlightenment, or nirvana, and use all or some of these as a center to hold together our understanding of facts and our experiences which do not of themselves fall into coherence, in spite of what Hegel's scheme proposed. The Designer of the Locks evidently decided on no such neat order, even if that intention is quite complex and was long in coming into our view. We can hold the world in perspective; but it does not do so of itself. We can sometimes enlighten ourselves, find the keys for locks which were long held shut against the mind. But we now know that we have achieved this only in part. We often see through the glass held up to Nature, but never as face to face, only in shades of dark and light.

Chapter VIII. THE ARGUMENT FOR GOD AT THE END OF THE 20TH CENTURY

A. Based on the Impossibility of any Total, Final Explanation of an Unstable World.

Ironic, is it not, that the very expectation at the start of our century, that man should be the focus of attention and not God, since we could explain the world's origins and future from our own investigations into Nature, thank you -- that this should reverse itself at the end of the century and become a new not-here-to-fore-imagined argument for the need of a creative divinity in our explanation of Nature. This is precisely because no necessity can be found for the emergence of worlds, universes, or human nature with its cultures and its atrocities, at least not as derived from a simple understanding of Nature's present structure.

We once thought we needed a God, or gods, to explain both why we were here and where we came from, as well as where we might be going and how we should live en route. As cultures proliferated, as science expanded and as technologies brought us closer to controlling what we thought to be vast creative powers, Prometheus (now demythologized into a human success story) became our symbol and our revolutionary cry. We did not need to have God creating at our start, at our origins, since now we held in our own hands the power to recreate ourselves and our societies.

Why, we now justifiably ask, was this Modern script not played out as written? We walk on the moon and live in space, as we have neither seen nor heard of any god doing. Why, once we had dismissed God from the human scene as no longer needed, as an illusion who's future had been called, as Freud put it -- why should any God, even if radically reconceived, be reintroduced when so much of our optimism over human control and knowledge and power (witness Hiroshima) has been confirmed? Adam and Eve could neither imagine our advance nor conceive of our takeover of the whole tree of knowledge, vs. their relatively innocent eating of a single apple.

Why the gods/Gods return? It is due to the rise to prominence in our 20th century experience of uncertainty, chance, terror, destruction and chaos. It is the unexpected endings to the century that allows a divine re-entry. All has not come out as the Enlightenment projected. Modern optimism over our ability to rewrite the script for humanity's future, one which was more favorable than any earlier religious scripture, has proved at best uncertain. In *The Deputy* you recall the prisoner saying defiantly to the vicious guard: "Because you exist, God also exists." That is, even the horror of a holocaust's destruction still does not seem to destroy all that lives. Israel exists, although it does so under constant fire and controversy. Why does human life survive our clumsy or brutal attempts to destroy our own kind?

Our history and our future now appear so uncertain, so precarious, and we have proved to be so capable of defeating "the best laid plans of mice and men" that we are forced to wonder, not only how we first arrived on the scene according to Darwin's Plot, but how we have managed to survive our own tendency to self-destruct, both psychologically and physically, and yet emerge in occasional triumph. So much could have thwarted our advance that the very uncertainty, and the chance element we sense in our past and in our future, argues not to a controlling but to a contingent power of choice.

The God who can -- not must -- emerge for the 21st century is not the God of necessity, not even one governed by science (in its original Modern sense) or by the precision of mathematical logic. Computerized our next divinity may be, yet chaos appears frequently on the heavenly command center screens. Frequent adjustments must be made to keep the whole drama from achieving a tragic and a sudden ending. Freedom and individual choice appear everywhere to throw off all hope of rigid predictions, thus requiring constant readjustment even of those decisions once thought firmly and even eternally in divine control.

We know from our own postmodern experience that no achieved form or expression is inherently stable. Any insight we value or produce needs effort to maintain itself. All order and accomplishment can become Yugoslavia; all human love and compassion turn into a killing field. How and why, we marvel today, could or did any stability ever emerge, human intelligence and creativity ever discover and sustain any value, given the constant closeness of our age to primitive and unconscious struggle. The wars we hoped would end all wars, the utopias we had good reason to think we could establish, the control of nature's vast forces we thought within our reach -- these ideals still attract us. But they are too often violated by terror for us to believe that they could hold the key to our future.

Ironically, our intelligent existence appears more precarious, more vulnerable to loss, than the Medieval Age which we so hurriedly sought to exit. Religious belief became a hindrance which Modern optimism sought to reject. Why believe in God's control when we could provide our own explanations, determine our own future? 'Belief' became an object of derision, a weakness which men -- and some women -- would overcome. But we had not counted on the emergence of contingency, our increased sense of the precariousness of life, of terror and of violence, plus our failure to escape our inhumanity to all that is human.

What gives life its stability, if we cannot trust ourselves as a human race? What allows order to arise out of constantly present chaos, not simply by the original ordering recorded in Genesis 1:1? What force holds vulnerable progress away from degeneration? No necessity, no simple logos or force of reason can accomplish this. But then, can a constant, renewed divine creativity? -- perhaps. An adaptable power of sufficient control to counterbalance our foibles, to bring life continually anew out of destruction? God is needed not simply once but constantly to offer continual revisions to Nature's, and to our unstable, manner of control. There is no final reading of Nature's advance, only eternal adjustments to keep our primeval freedom from running out of control.

Is such a God who can appear in the 21st century sufficient to support religious belief, however much this must be constantly revised? No final de-mythologizing is possible, since myth is itself basic to all creativity. But new non-empirical, non-visible, symbolic renderings of the divine must be offered. The vast speculation of our late 20th century science, vs. the fixity and unity of scientific theory we once sought (and is still sought by many too nostalgic to surrender the dream) -- all this leads us to feel the need for a stabilizing, a vastly powerful center, which Nature does not provide from itself and which cannot seem to emerge from our attempts to finalize theory. This belief, this hope, replaces the certainty which we once thought would inevitably come.

The command center needed to launch missions into space is modest indeed compared to what God must need if any balance is to be maintained among the forces at loose in our world, both physical and human. The God above time, divinity at rest, is useless to our needs in the 21st century, however satisfying such deity may have been to Aristotle, Augustine, or Aquinas. The God drawing us above time to monastic and serene contemplation is "gone with the wind", a divinity not able to emerge and to sustain itself in our consciousness now.

Does this make any religious story, any recommended religious practice or observance, whether Christian, Buddhist, Confucius or Muslim, acceptable to sophisticated thinkers, just as able to be believed now as it once seemed necessary to reject each religion in the name of the Enlightenment and Scientific advance? Not necessarily, but then little in the 21st century offers us any necessity. Yet contingently and freely, various pictures of divinity's power of control may reemerge. The divine freedom can be deduced from ours, although the difference is that we now project that our emerging deity uses -- or at least will eventually use -- its power for good, as much as possible, whereas human power, however great, never escapes the split into good and evil.

In the 21st century we can only be surprised by God. Of course, we always have been surprised by divinities, but we have not always recognized this, preferring in our classic utopian dreams to have God under our control, i.e., offering us no surprises. But any divinity able to keep up with, let alone create, universes and peoples as complex and unstable as we and our planets are, must by nature be surprising. Imagine God in this world of holocaust and terror and destruction, incarnating a divinity with a message that the creator-God is loving, compassionate and forgiving. That is enough to make one laugh hysterically, given the chaos in the hate-filled world we see around us so often at war with itself. That claim may be true, of course, but if so it is the ultimate surprise. "Surely, you're joking Mr. Fineman", applies to God as well as to unorthodox physicists. Should the God who created chaos and life with uncertainty prove to be loving, what could be a greater surprise? Imagine, sacrificing himself for us!

How odd of God to claim to offer love to all humanity, good and evil alike. And if true, we can resign ourselves to the fact that we will never resolve our relationship to that divine into security and finality. God must not want that, and certainly the design of the world's evolution does not argue for fixity. We have blocked our own path to God by demanding impossible things. We demand security, finality. Divinity promises resolution, but not yet. Wait. Be patient. Be at work. Follow the path of exploration. Be steady in our agonizing descent and in the divine silence. And has God emerged more of recent, although it has not as yet been realized by many? How? Where? In the uncertainty, in the contingency and in the terror into which we have all been tossed. We had projected utopia, scientific understandings, final comprehension. That has not come, but God's true nature is perhaps more to be felt in this disappointment than in our humanistic optimism.

God has surprised us by not being where we expected, by not standing still to provide our security and then simply establishing religious rituals and churches. In this lack of finality, which we must now accept as our human situation, can no religious promise be believed? Will the messiah never come for the devout Jew, the one so long awaited? Of course, a God of surprises and uncertainty, one who allows no finality, can appear at any time or place. But such an emerging God cannot be coerced, cannot be forced. Can such an uncertain divinity not incarnate himself in Jesus and suffer terror and hatred and death, as we do? Certainly, but such an act can never cease to be surprising and startling and unexpected, plus the fact that God can and did withdraw again. And divinity has established no completion date for the promised salvation, since the world itself and human nature remain incomplete too. Can the unexplained God give revelations to Mohammed or to Joseph Smith? Certainly, but they will be surprising, disclosures not full of absolute guarantees, unless we try to pin God down by merely using our words. God, oddly, often allows us to overspeak, to overcommit divinity -- but we must take the responsibility for doing that, not God.

What can our human religious response be to any such announced uncertain truth? Accept it as true, but recognize it as uncertain. What should our individual responses be? Belief, since certainty is inappropriate? Should our religious life be full of surprises? Yes, certainly. That is our only certainty, if we understand how to relate to a 21st century emerging deity. Happy, calm, serene, loving, compassionate? Yes, all of those, if we will. Yet the created order not only does not demand this; it in fact works against such a response. Any religious person is just as unusual in this world as the deity is surprising. Life like that is exciting and overwhelming, but only if we realize and accept how unusual, how unorthodox, all true religion and science and creativity must be if it seeks to be honest.

B. NOT THE END OF HISTORY, BUT THE END OF UTOPIAS

Francis Fukuyama created a bit of a stir, in intellectual circles at least, by proclaiming "the end of history." Edward Mortimer, in his article in *The Financial Times**, thinks our struggles will not end in any case, even if there is a new world order, as President Bush proclaimed. Following the resurgence of non-Western cultures and the decline of the dominance of Western democratic values, Samuel Huntington in *Foreign Affairs*, predicted that future conflicts will come primarily between civilizations ("The Clash of Civilizations?",

---

* "Has the West Triumphed at Last?" 1 January '94, weekend, p.1.

as quoted by Mortimer). Yet perhaps none of the observers of our future have quite noted the surprising decline, in fact the virtual disappearance, of the various utopian ideals (dreams?) which captured Western imaginations for so long. They became accepted almost as truth/fact by many, one version of which played a hand in founding the United States.

Hegel is also utopian in his outline of the dialectic of history, since he builds his program on progress and on increasing world integration. In the sense of Hegel's dramatic picture of history's rational movement toward a climax, we perhaps have come to the end of our belief in that sort of 'history', but obviously not the end of all history. Of course, Hegel's dialectic of history was built on conflict; in fact struggle required loss in order to proceed. So even if his views of progression toward utopia are no longer widely believed, our struggles will not end, as Mortimer reminds us. But to many, the United States has epitomized, at least for most of its own citizens, "the best of the West", and we are so utopian in our own self-vision that such dreams have been hard to dispel. Oddly, this is as true abroad as it is within the US, in spite of numerous vocal critiques of our policy and our culture. The disappearance of Marxism may best symbolize this. Neither the USSR nor the US really understand that both were built on utopian visions of achieving a new life and the opportunity free of old restraints. Thus, the disappearance of the attraction of the Marxist utopia is at the same time the demise of American utopian visions.

Why necessarily so? Certainly a majority of residents in "the states" felt that their self-vision, which was attractive to millions as expressed in the Declaration of Independence and in the Constitution, were "beacons set upon a hill", a light unto the world, whereas Russia represented repression. Leaving aside the economic issue of Capitalism vs. Communism, or even strict socialism, why cannot the utopian visions of the Founding Fathers now march forward to victory, no matter what the rest of the world wants to do?

Because the Civil War and the Civil Rights movements told us that our dreams contained major, perhaps even disastrous, flaws. Can we not correct these, as many idealists hoped? Not if the drift into an uneducated and an economically powerless Underclass continues to build up in our inner cities. Our youth, who live and struggle there, are not entranced by a utopian future. The rise of violence, so little predictable when the Pilgrims landed at Plymouth Rock, makes utopias hard to envision, since violence is not the road there unto.

At our chauvinistic and imperialistic heights, we have chided Asian cultures, philosophies, and religions for not offering their people a vision of Utopian Progress. Now, whether we admit it or not, few residents in the fifty states any longer believe in a 'progress' view of history. They may like the culture of Texas or the life style of Hawaii, but few really connect that to "bringing forth on this content" a really new nation. Again, why? Because our economy, our security, even our culture, is not and cannot be cut off by the Atlantic and Pacific. The terrors of all the world are our terrors; and they are just as likely to strike us at home as abroad.

Americans, all Westerners, no longer have any place to hide. Or, if we try to do so, our economies will perish. We are committed inter-nationalists, like it or not. US. isolationism was in many ways a happy dream, but as an option it has faded even faster than our utopian founding visions. Western science, technology, even values, might they not still lead the way, just as the rapid press to develop technologies all over the world might cause us to flatter ourselves as world leaders? Maybe. But dominance, success in these areas does not seem to be the exclusive domain of any culture or continent. Whatever economic or military power anyone possesses, none of these today can be wielded or controlled exclusively by any one nation or religion or culture. East was East and West was West, but they have now met and passed each other. We may or may not understand our world neighbors any better than Boston understands Dallas, but we are inevitably linked.

We are not a "global village," that ultimate oxymoron. In spite of communication superhighways and space-age travel, we are incredibly more chaotic and diverse, if not outright weird at times, in our contrasts. Smallpox and cannibalism may have been eradicated, but all the world's religions and all our varying ethical systems seem no closer to amalgamation now than before the world-wide Christian missionary movement. A few intellectuals from various cultures and religions can meet and find some common ground in words, but the average native of any country or member of any ethnic group seems to show a greater tendency to hatred than to reconciliation, in spite of an occasional and welcome counter example. To know the cultures and religions of the world is not necessarily to love them; far from it, according to what CNN shows us.

Fukuyama argued that the superior virtues of the West's political and economic freedom had finally been demonstrated by the crumbling of the Berlin wall. Following the Enlightenment notion of individual liberty, the US. is often in the lead. We could not see why anyone should desire anything else, unless they were untouched by enlightenment education. Yet we overlooked our human fascination with power and the attraction that exercising control holds for us. We failed to estimate just how many will fight and die to devastate their enemies. Hatreds did not cease, neither personal, ethnic, nor religious, and so wars do not cease. Tyrants, like suckers, are born every day, in any age or time, even if social restraints sometimes cause them to dress and to act differently in order to conceal their motives. Utopias of all types are crushed on the rock of our inability to change the basic forces of human nature, although these may be softened by education or religion or even by control and repression -- for a time.

'Egalitarianism' is popular today in many intellectual circles. The notion that we are all created equal, which obviously is false, and that we are all equally talented, goes so blatantly against our cultural behavior where "pop stars and sport stars are born," that it is hard to see how anyone can believe it, except as a dream. Thus, we see that the Utopia to which we must bid good-bye was unfortunately based on the equality of all, and so its last gasp is to try to continue to assert the equality of all in culture and in talent. As basic and important and unirradicable individual and cultural differences reassert themselves on a global scale, utopias come crashing down. We will not ever all be the same, except perhaps to have the same rights under certain, although not universal, legal systems, or perhaps in the eyes of God according to some admirable religious doctrines.

In the future we may live in one of two zones, either in a stable and rich democracy or in a zone of turmoil (*cf. The Real World Order* by Singer and Wildavsky). The problem is that, as we have argued, the world will never be so neatly divided, nor so stable, nor the time of transition between one to the other so long. Rapid change and instability characterize the worlds of physics, of economics, and of culture, and turmoil can arise internally as well as externally. Powerful, democratic states may no longer threaten each other with war, as has been argued, but the rest of the world will. And certainly our ability to establish peace by superior force has proved unsuccessful in Vietnam as well as in once beautiful Yugoslavia. Technical superiority may stay largely within democracies, but autocratic control still has amazing capabilities, all the while our Western uncontrolled freedom is hard to direct and thus is vulnerable to terrorism.

As Huntington's article pointed out, superiority will not reside predominantly with the West. Whether or not one argues that others have copied the Western democracies, certainly this is more true in technology than in democratic values. Kant's universally held morals do not hold as far away from Konigsburg as he thought, and certainly they are not implicit in all human reason. In fact, universality in almost any form, except in scientific and mathematical theories, is little likely to be accepted on an international scale and so cannot be assumed as a basis for discussion. We all, by a wide margin, do not accept any common set of values world wide, as much as we may wish to claim 'superiority' for Christian or Enlightenment value systems. One basis may still be arguably better than another, but no indigenous ingredient in human nature or cultures will be recognized by all who are human. And certainly not all women or people of any racial group will agree.

Decadence can infect any culture and any person, high or low, powerful or otherwise. Certainly, individually we can still go through self-cleansing and regeneration, even sometimes as whole cities and nations. Both power and purity are where you find them, and the ascent or the descent of cultures depends a great deal on their response to the challenges which confront them. Professor Chan Heng Chee of Singapore may be right: Not all see the adoption of Western 'liberal' models as the route to power and prominence. In fact, tight political and economic control often surmounts difficulties more easily, provided it does not turn to massive destruction or get locked into internal power struggles. On a worldwide scale, many will prefer to continue to fight for control rather than enter into dialogue and negotiations. Of course, centralized bureaucracies work better in smaller situations rather than in larger territories with vast ethnic and racial differences, unless backed by strong military power and repression.

Political democracy in itself is not enough to lead a country or a society, whether large or small, to success. A thousand other factors, many perhaps beyond our control, now enter in. And "natural resources" are no longer so plentiful so easily exploited in order to yield economic power and societal well being. Neither the division into West and East nor any other can be counted on to hold or to yield stability for very long, in our emerging common future.

Hegel thought that civilization would merge at first by clashing, of course. Yet philosophies and religions are not likely to become one, much as some desire this. Race, religion, and culture can sometimes be combined, as in Malaysia or in the United States. But the point is that nothing can be counted on to provide, or to sustain, peace and prosperity for very long any more. The utopias which so many in the West thought could be brought into being are, like the Old South in the U. S., "gone with the wind. "

Citizens of the United States have always, often to the disgust of other countries and cultures, considered themselves different from others and to be in possession of a special mission in the world. This crusade mentality has never been "all bad," since these same chauvinistic citizens have also opened their doors, often if not always, to the "huddled masses yearning to be free." To stand for equality and freedom for all is a needed symbol, even if at times it is denied by our actions and taken to extremes on other occasions. It has been said that the US. is today "the only truly international society in the world." The increase of new citizens arriving from Asia and Africa and South America has added a new dimension of diversity in our culture, but diversity itself is as old as our founding.

If we set our utopian visions behind us, can we still uncover a unique mission for ourselves in our brave new world? If we no longer allow ourselves to act as if we are superior to men and women from other nations, can we still strive to show that a broad spread of cultures and peoples can live and work together and succeed in peace? Accepting ourselves as fallible men and women, just like all who have come before us, possessing no magic formula to eliminate human fault, can we still work to achieve a unity from among the many? Yes, we can operate around the globe, not always by imposing our values but rather by seeking to work for the good of all and not simply for ourselves, fallible human being that we know we are. The revival tents which brought a once pagan South to religious conversion can once again preach a new, but less provincial, 'gospel' of human cooperation, but one not premised on the impossible merger of all cultures into one.

POSTSCRIPT: To Speak The Truth, To Write The Truth

Can this be done? Yes, but not in so many words. It may "come forth" in the interplay of ideas and in the serious mind's struggle. Yet this can happen only from time to time. 'Truth' itself may be eternal, but it does not appear to us as such, nor can it be passed from person to person in any assured or fixed way. Having read Wittgenstein, does God at least think that divinities may speak or write the truth, describe even the Mystical, in divinity's ordinary language? Not directly but only indirectly, in that the divine mind knows in how many ways truth may be perceived, how it may be put in forms so that, with skill and devotion, truth can be "read off" by other minds, such as designs for the construction of universes or of the smallest particles. Unlike the divine, the human mind is another matter, since it is even more complex and hidden at times, manifesting itself more clearly physically than psychologically. In contrast, the divine will is free in its constructed expressions; our minds and words must overcome restraints to speak at all clearly. Often this "happening" is what we preserve momentarily in all classics of literature, art, or song.

But for God truth is held in view by the divine will and the divine power. This is a much more reliable and steady instrument and force than its human counterpart, except as the few are occasionally inspired. What we achieve through hard labor and years of collective effort (as Aristotle thought possible), the divine intelligence holds calmly open to its view, except as it rotates its massive kaleidoscope to achieve various perspectives and to disclose added intricacies. At our worst, humans are destructive, of themselves and even of their acquired knowledge. Libraries are easily burned. At our best, we approach the ways in which God views the world, and occasionally we even have glimpses of the divine life. But this is rare, not long sustained, not fixed beyond time (it cannot be if it is 'true'), not even single in divinity's perspective as Spinoza hoped it would be. Computers can simulate some aspects of God's super-speed intellect, but they mirror neither its most subtle aspects nor its mercurial dependence on the divine will.

Thus, it is an exaggeration of our powers to think that we have the ability simply "to speak the truth" -- on any but the most trivial questions -- or that our minds are subtle enough to apprehend truth by virtue of their own inborn skill. Insights come; they are sometimes written down. Yet often they lie dormant until focused on by another diligent and persevering soul. But all too frequently they are either overlooked or misused. For a time 'truth' was thought to be recordable and transmittable in scientific discourse, particularly if mathematically expressed. But as scientific theories soar in their speculative ranges in their non-observability and then pass at their furthest reaches out of normal sight by any direct means, it is an oversimplification to say that scientific theory itself "states the truth".

In their compressed simplicity, the best words, the best theories, lead us to insight just as poetry does. Average words and expressions, ordinary language, seldom do. But all insights into truth retain an 'esoteric' quality vs. the 'exoteric' phrasing the Modern world hoped all truth could achieve. And if it cannot be shared directly by all or expressed by all, the desired democracy of truth flies out the window. At best, we are left with a "representative democracy" of truth. Acknowledged experts whom we elect by careful discrimination are capable of dealing subtly with truth possibilities. Like the Sibyl in ancient Greece, we acknowledge some exceptional individuals; we inspire them to make statements and theories which they find fascinating to utter. They become our elected spokespersons of truth.

God, then, must struggle to reduce truth to acceptable forms even for exceptional human comprehension, although it is the divine intention to make this available only in small amounts, seldom in large quantities, and never totally. The divine nature may retain its mysterious, its partially inexpressible qualities, in itself. But in relation to us, God has refocused truth's configuration so that it can be present in exceptional expressions on a human scale as well. Yet God must struggle to do this, since our ways are not the divine ways of thought, and truth always contains a contingent element of time-relationship. There can be no divine expression of truth that is time-free and culture-free. If the recent doctrine of 'deconstruction' means that, then it is quite accurate. If it means that truth has no core, then, it goes against our instinct which is to preserve what we know to be more lasting than cultural fashion, to extract truth from its fashionable dress.

We can sometimes write the truth, and we should never stop trying to do so. We should just take up our pens (or our computers or our cameras) knowing how difficult, and thus how rare, it is to accomplish. In writing or in speaking, we are often unable to distinguish the important, and thus the potentially lasting, utterances from the fashions of the moment. Occasionally, truth falls into words, into art, into act, but not so that all must acknowledge it as such. It does not appear "*in* so many words", in a stone, in a gesture, but it can appear *through* them. It is our challenge, as speakers, as creators, as actors, to accomplish this transfiguration, this epiphany. Recognition is sometimes, but only infrequently, immediate. We write, we speak, we act for the reader, for our immediate audience, but often we must wait for the citizen yet unborn. Truth seeks out our posterity, leaving the pioneers to possess it, aware of having apprehended it, but only rarely other than in an uncertain form.

INDEX